Women With Adhd

A Life-changing Guide to Overcoming Distractions

(A Guide on What to Do and How to Love Your Partner Better)

Harry Walker

Published By **Harriet Parker**

Harry Walker

Women With Adhd: A Life-changing Guide to Overcoming Distractions (A Guide on What to Do and How to Love Your Partner Better)

ISBN   978-1-7781462-2-0

No part of this guidebook shall be reproduced in any form without permission in writing from the publisher except in the case of brief quotations embodied in critical articles or reviews.

Legal & Disclaimer

The information contained in this book is not designed to replace or take the place of any form of medicine or professional medical advice. The information in this book has been provided for educational & entertainment purposes only.

The information contained in this book has been compiled from sources deemed reliable, and it is accurate to the best of the Author's knowledge; however, the Author cannot guarantee its accuracy and validity and cannot be held liable for any errors or omissions. Changes are periodically made to this book. You must consult your doctor or get professional medical advice before using any of the suggested remedies, techniques, or information in this book.

Table Of Contents

Chapter 1: What Is Adhd?

The neurodevelopment ailment called Attention Deficit Hyperactivity Disorder (ADHD) is typified by using impulsivity, hyperactivity, and inattention. Although this illness can persist into adulthood, it is maximum commonly diagnosed in youngsters. ADHD impacts an anticipated 8.Four% of youngsters and a pair of.Five% of adults within the United States.

ADHD is a complex sickness that impacts a person's functionality to govern their behavior, interest, and pay interest. People with ADHD have problem focusing on responsibilities, staying organized, and dealing with time. They may also moreover have trouble controlling their emotions and impulses. Symptoms of ADHD can variety in severity and can intervene with someone's capacity to function in everyday life.

Common signs and symptoms and signs and symptoms of ADHD embody inattentiveness, hyperactivity, and impulsivity. Inattentiveness can get up as trouble being attentive to info, problem following commands, trouble staying centered, and problem organizing tasks. Hyperactivity can get up as fidgeting, speaking excessively, and problem staying seated. Impulsivity can arise as trouble geared up turns, blurting out answers, and interrupting conversations. ADHD is diagnosed by way of the use of a intellectual fitness professional primarily based on an assessment of signs and symptoms and symptoms and signs and symptoms and behavior. There isn't always any single check that can diagnose ADHD, and evaluation is primarily based mostly on a entire evaluation of someone's behavior. Treatment alternatives for ADHD consist of medication, psychotherapy, manner of existence adjustments, and academic accommodations.

ADHD is a complicated ailment that could have a good sized impact on a person's lifestyles. It is essential to trying to find remedy as quickly as viable if you want to assist control signs and enhance functioning. With the proper help and interventions, human beings with ADHD can prevail and attain their complete ability.

Who is laid low with ADHD

Children with ADHD often have trouble in college, as they may battle to interest at the teacher's training, complete homework assignments, or have interaction with other college students. They may also be greater vulnerable to moving into hassle with disruptive conduct, which include talking out of flip or being disruptive in splendor. Adults with ADHD might also have problem retaining relationships, dealing with finances, or retaining a assignment. ADHD can get up in each genders, however it is extra commonplace in adult men than ladies. It is likewise greater not unusual amongst children than adults. While ADHD can occur at any age, it's miles maximum usually recognized in children some of the some time of 6 and 12.

ADHD have to have a big effect at the lives of these tormented by it. It can cause problem in faculty, art work, relationships, and social situations. People with ADHD can also war with low conceitedness, melancholy, tension, and substance abuse.

However, with proper remedy, people with ADHD can lead a success lives. Treatment normally includes a combination of medication and psychosocial interventions, which consist of behavior exchange, treatment, and schooling. Treatment can assist to reduce the signs and symptoms and symptoms of ADHD and enhance functioning. ADHD influences loads of loads of people in the United States, along with youngsters and adults. With right treatment, humans with ADHD can lead a hit and inexperienced lives.

ADHD in Women

Women with ADHD regularly revel in disturbing situations that are taken into consideration one in every of a type from men with the disorder. For instance, ladies may also additionally have hassle with government functioning, together with time manage, business agency, and multitasking. Women can also have problems with emotional law, main to feelings of immoderate unhappiness or irritability. In addition, ladies with ADHD often have trouble with social abilities, which encompass interacting with others and attractive in nonverbal communication.

Women with ADHD are also more likely to have coexisting situations, which includes tension, despair, and eating problems. These coexisting situations can worsen signs and symptoms and signs and make it greater tough to control ADHD. Women with ADHD also can enjoy unique demanding situations inside the place of business. They may additionally moreover have trouble with duties that require sustained hobby, collectively with completing opinions or staying targeted within the path of meetings. Women may also furthermore discover it tough to undergo in mind data or take a look at thru on duties. As a give up end result, girls can be perceived as disorganized or now not taking their task significantly.

Fortunately, there are remedies to be had for women with ADHD. Stimulant drug remedies, which includes Adderall and Ritalin, can assist enhance interest and decrease impulsivity. Non-stimulant drug remedies, along aspect Strattera, also may be powerful. Cognitive behavioral therapy (CBT) can help girls with ADHD have a look at techniques to manipulate their signs, which includes growing better organizational capabilities and enhancing verbal exchange.

Chapter 2: Understanding Treatment Options

Attention Deficit Hyperactivity Disorder (ADHD) is a highbrow illness that influences masses and thousands of human beings worldwide. It is a chronic state of affairs that can be tough to control, and it is able to have diverse outcomes on a person's life. For older women, the assessment and remedy of ADHD may be especially difficult, due to the reality the symptoms and signs and goals of this population may also variety from those of extra younger humans. In this article, we will speak the severa remedy alternatives to be had for older girls with ADHD, which encompass lifestyle modifications, medicines, and mental interventions.

Lifestyle modifications are one of the maximum essential elements of handling ADHD in older ladies. These changes can assist to lessen symptoms and signs and signs and symptoms and enhance regular functioning in each day sports activities. For example, retaining a regular sleep time table, project ordinary bodily pastime, and preserving off caffeine and other stimulants can all assist to lessen hyperactivity and impulsivity in older girls with ADHD. Additionally, breaking down responsibilities into smaller, more viable steps and the use of organizational gear can assist to enhance attention and awareness. Medications also are an powerful treatment preference for older women with ADHD. Stimulant medicinal drugs, which consist of methylphenidate and amphetamine, are the most usually prescribed drugs for ADHD. These medicinal drugs art work by way of the usage of way of developing degrees of dopamine and norepinephrine, which might be neurotransmitters which can be related to popularity and interest. Non-stimulant drugs, inclusive of atomoxetine and guanfacine, also are to be had and can be used to deal with ADHD symptoms and signs in older humans.

In addition to medicinal tablets, intellectual interventions can also be beneficial for older girls with ADHD. These interventions can encompass cognitive-behavioral treatment (CBT) and psychotherapy, that can assist individuals to amplify higher coping strategies for managing their symptoms. Additionally, family remedy may be useful for supporting older ladies with ADHD to expand better communique and problem-fixing talents.

Medications

ADHD medicinal drugs are available essential instructions: stimulants and non-stimulants. Stimulants, which includes methylphenidate (Ritalin) and amphetamines (Adderall), are taken into consideration the simplest pills for ADHD. These medicinal capsules paintings speedy to enhance cognizance and attention, reduce impulsivity, and help with time management.

Non-stimulants, which includes atomoxetine (Strattera) and bupropion (Wellbutrin), moreover may be used to cope with ADHD. These medicinal drugs work greater slowly than stimulants, however can be the favored treatment for older girls because of their decrease danger of facet outcomes.

In addition to stimulants and non-stimulants, there are high-quality medicinal drugs that can be used to cope with ADHD. These medicinal capsules encompass tricyclic antidepressants, anticonvulsants, antipsychotics, and alpha-2 agonists. Each of these capsules has specific effects at the body, and it's critical to talk about the professionals and cons of every on the side of your medical doctor earlier than starting treatment.

In addition to medicinal capsules, way of lifestyles changes also can assist manage

ADHD signs in older ladies. Strategies such as mindfulness, exercise, and right sleep hygiene can help reduce signs and enhance first-rate of life. Learning stress control skills and placing inexpensive dreams also may be beneficial.

It's additionally vital to be conscious that pills aren't the awesome manner to manage ADHD signs and signs. Cognitive-behavioral treatment (CBT) can help adults with ADHD manipulate their signs and beautify their excellent of life. CBT can help adults pick out out and trade behavior which can be contributing to their signs and symptoms and signs and signs and teach them strategies to higher manipulate their ADHD. ADHD drug treatments may be an effective manner to control signs and signs in older women. With the proper remedy and way of lifestyles modifications, older girls can enhance their awareness, organisation, and everyday super of life.

Therapy

ADHD is most customarily identified in youngsters and youngsters, it may also be determined in maturity. Women over the age of 40 are particularly vulnerable to developing ADHD, because of hormonal modifications and one in every of a type lifestyles occasions. ADHD treatment for older ladies is an crucial part of remedy for this situation. ADHD remedy allows ladies benefit belief into the signs and signs and symptoms and symptoms and behaviors related to ADHD, and boom strategies to higher manipulate them. With the assist of a certified therapist, women can research useful coping competencies, which encompass the manner to better control their time, prioritize obligations, and stay prepared.

Therapy also can help women come to be privy to patterns of their conduct that is a cease bring about their ADHD. For instance, women may additionally discover that they procrastinate loads, or that they have got difficulty staying focused on duties. By getting to know the way to apprehend those styles and boom techniques to govern them, women can enhance their functioning and everyday exceptional of existence. ADHD remedy for older girls also focuses on helping them manipulate the emotional and social factors of the disorder. Women with ADHD can regularly enjoy overwhelmed, remoted, or misunderstood. Therapy can assist them advantage self-interest and increase extremely good coping techniques to address the ones problems.

Therapy also can help ladies with ADHD gather higher relationships with circle of relatives and pals. Women regularly locate that their relationships go through due to their ADHD signs. With the help of a certified therapist, ladies can learn how to higher communicate their dreams and interact in healthful techniques with their loved ones. ADHD remedy for older ladies can assist enhance common nice of lifestyles and functioning. With the help of a certified therapist, women can learn how to manipulate their symptoms and emerge as extra on top of things of their lives. In addition to traditional communicate treatment, there are a number of one-of-a-type treatments that can be used to help address ADHD in older ladies. These include:

Cognitive-behavioral remedy (CBT): CBT allows women become aware of and assignment terrible mind and behaviors that would contribute to ADHD symptoms and symptoms and symptoms.

Mindfulness-based totally absolutely remedy: Mindfulness-primarily based treatment enables girls emerge as greater privy to their thoughts and emotions, and increase strategies to better control them.

Neurofeedback: Neurofeedback uses EEG (electroencephalograph) technology to assist girls emerge as more aware about their mind hobby, and learn how to higher modify it.

Art treatment: Art treatment allows women explicit themselves in a revolutionary way, and might help them advantage insights into their behaviors and feelings.

Exercise treatment: Exercise is an important a part of ADHD remedy, and might help ladies gain more manipulate over their signs and symptoms and signs and symptoms.

Diet and nutrients remedy: A healthy food regimen and nutrients plan can assist lessen ADHD signs and signs and symptoms, and can also improve famous physical and mental health.

Medication: Medications additionally can be used to help manipulate ADHD signs, even though they need to continuously be used on the thing of various treatment alternatives.

Chapter 3: Managing Adhd

Exercise has been verified to be an effective tool for managing ADHD signs and symptoms in each adults and children. For older ladies, who may be managing the symptoms of ADHD, exercise can be particularly useful. Exercise can assist enhance awareness, recognition, and agency organisation, in addition to lessen strain, tension, and fatigue.

Regular bodily hobby can assist reduce hyperactivity and decorate impulsivity, not unusual symptoms of ADHD. Exercise can also help enhance everyday cognitive functioning and stimulate the release of endorphins, hormones which could assist lessen strain and enhance temper. Exercise can also assist decorate sleep excellent, which may be specifically beneficial for humans with ADHD.

For older ladies with ADHD, it's far crucial to find out an workout routine that is every fun and effective. Low-impact sports which encompass strolling, swimming, and yoga may be extraordinary alternatives for offering bodily hobby and strain consolation. Strength training is likewise beneficial as it can assist enhance stability, coordination, and muscle strength.

It is also important to recognition on consistency at the same time as growing an workout regular. Regular physical interest is maximum beneficial on the identical time as it's miles completed on a steady foundation, so it's miles vital to set a intention and keep on with it. It is also essential to discover a ordinary that is flexible and clean to in shape into your schedule. Examples of sporting occasions which could help manage the symptoms of ADHD in older ladies consist of walking, swimming, yoga, and energy schooling.

Walking is a incredible manner to get bodily interest and may help to lessen stress and beautify attention. Swimming is also a low-effect interest which could help to reduce hyperactivity and enhance impulsivity.

Yoga is a terrific way to alleviate stress, enhance balance and coordination, and increase flexibility. Strength schooling is also beneficial as it can help to enhance muscle electricity and reduce fatigue.

It is essential to interest on consistency on the equal time as growing an exercise habitual. Regular bodily interest is maximum useful even as it's far completed on a normal foundation, so it's far crucial to set a cause and preserve on with it. It is also crucial to discover a habitual that is bendy and clean to in form into a while table. When starting an exercising habitual, it's far vital to start slowly and often increase depth and duration. It's crucial to be aware of your frame's indicators and save you if you revel in any pain or pain. Lastly, it's miles essential to don't forget to stay hydrated and fuel your body with wholesome snacks and meals.

10 Exercise Strategies for Managing ADHD Symptoms in older women

1. Try precise sports activities activities – Variety is crucial as regards to exercising, so it's miles essential to attempt fantastic sports activities to find out what works high-quality for you.

2. Set sensible desires – Set realistic desires which can be conceivable and unique. It's critical to prioritize improvement above perfection.

3. Take breaks – Take ordinary breaks in some unspecified time in the future of your exercise ordinary to prevent fatigue and harm.

four. Exercise with a chum – Exercising with a chum can help to keep you inspired and accountable.

five. Find a supportive surroundings – Find an environment that is supportive and scary. This can assist to preserve you endorsed and decrease pressure.

6. Track your development – Track your progress as you visit assist stay induced and feature amusing your successes.

7. Reward your self – Celebrate your successes through profitable your self with a few issue unique.

8. Exercise regularly: Regular exercising can assist beautify recognition, reduce pressure and tension, and enhance temper. Try to exercise for at the least 1/2 of an hour each day.

nine. Join a health elegance: Joining a health beauty together with yoga, Pilates, or aerobics can be a super manner to live triggered and get in some exercise.

10. Take a walk: Taking a every day stroll out of doors can assist clean your thoughts and get your heart charge up.

11. Do energy schooling: Strength education can assist lessen pressure, decorate popularity and hobby, and boom conceitedness.

12. Play a recreation: Playing a recreation together with tennis, basketball, or football can assist beautify coordination and interest.

13. Take up a hobby: Taking up a interest along with gardening, painting, or pix can help reduce pressure and provide a innovative outlet.

14. Listen to song: Listening to track could have a relaxing effect and can offer an first rate distraction from racing mind.

15. Practice mindfulness: Mindfulness sports along with meditation and deep

breathing can help beautify consciousness and reduce strain.

10 examples of the physical video games for women with ADHD

1. Walking: Walking is a high-quality low-effect workout that can assist enhance awareness, lessen stress and tension, and raise temper.

2. Running: Running is a wonderful manner to get your heart rate up and get an remarkable cardiovascular exercise.

3. Swimming: Swimming is a remarkable low-effect form of workout which can provide an superb cardiovascular workout.

four. Cycling: Cycling is a extraordinary way to get a few workout at the identical time as exploring the outdoors.

five. Yoga: Yoga can help improve flexibility and energy, lessen stress, and improve attention and popularity.

6. Pilates: Pilates can assist enhance posture, stability, and versatility.

7. Strength training: Strength training can help decorate energy and muscle tone and can beautify vanity.

8. Tai Chi: Tai Chi is a form of martial arts that may assist beautify balance, coordination, and attention.

9. Dance: Dance is a high-quality way to get some exercising whilst having a laugh.

10. Martial Arts: Martial arts can help enhance hobby, coordination, and self-control.

Sleep hygiene as a method to govern ADHD Sleep hygiene is a set of habits and practices which is probably designed to sell higher sleep. It consists of sports activities sports which incorporates placing a normal sleep time table, warding off caffeine and alcohol, workout often, and keeping off displays within the bed room. Sleep hygiene is crucial for every person, but in particular for humans with ADHD, as awful sleep can exacerbate signs and symptoms and signs. It can help lessen pressure and anxiety, modify the body's circadian rhythm, and sell higher sleep. Good sleep hygiene conduct can assist to enhance interest, awareness, and large intellectual health.

Sleep hygiene strategies for coping with ADHD symptoms and signs and symptoms in older girls consist of:

1. Establish a ordinary sleep schedule: Establishing a ordinary sleep time table can help alter the body's circadian rhythm and promote higher sleep. Going to bed and waking up at the equal time each day, even on weekends, can assist hold the body in a regular sleep pattern.

2. Avoid caffeine, alcohol, and nicotine: Caffeine, alcohol, and nicotine can all interfere with sleep, so it's miles essential to keep away from the ones materials inside

the night and past due at night time time time.

3. Exercise often: Regular exercising can help lessen stress and anxiety, that may help sell higher sleep. Aim for at the least half-hour of slight-intensity exercise severa instances consistent with week.

4. Avoid big meals earlier than mattress: Eating a massive meal close to bedtime can intervene with sleep. Try to consume a light snack or drink a tumbler of heat milk in advance than bedtime alternatively.

5. Create a calming bedtime habitual: A interesting bedtime regular can assist sign the body that it's time to sleep. This should embody taking a warmth bath, reading a e-book, or taking note of clean song.

6. Get sunlight hours exposure in the course of the day: Sunlight exposure at some degree inside the day can help alter the frame's circadian rhythm and sell higher

sleep. Aim to get at least half of-hour of daylight each day, if possible.

7. Avoid shows inside the mattress room: Screens together with TVs, computer structures, and phones can intervene with sleep. Try to limit show display use inside the bedroom, or turn off all devices at the least an hour earlier than bedtime.

eight. Make the bed room a nap-selling surroundings: The bed room have to be darkish, quiet, and funky. Consider making an investment in blackout curtains, a legitimate machine, or a fan to help sell higher sleep. Following those sleep hygiene strategies can assist manage ADHD symptoms in older women and sell higher sleep.

Dieting Strategy for Managing ADHD Symptoms in older women

1. Eat a balanced eating regimen with lots of easy quit stop end result, veggies, and complete grains: Eating a balanced weight-

reduction plan this is rich in culmination, greens, and complete grains can help to offer critical nutrients and minerals that can help to enhance signs and signs and symptoms of ADHD in older girls. Additionally, it's far essential to restriction processed foods, subtle sugars, and bad fat that can contribute to hyperactivity and irritability.

2. Incorporate omega-three fatty acids: Research has tested that omega-3 fatty acids can help to beautify symptoms and symptoms and signs of ADHD in older women, which include impulsivity and interest. Omega-three fatty acids may be found in fish, nuts, and great seeds.

3. Limit caffeine: Caffeine can exacerbate ADHD symptoms and signs and symptoms, so it's far essential to limit the amount of caffeine consumption.

four. Increase protein consumption: Increasing the quantity of protein within the food regimen can help to beautify attention and focus. Protein-wealthy meals embody nuts, beans, fish, lean meats, and eggs.

five. Eat food frequently: Eating ordinary meals inside the route of the day can assist to modify blood sugar tiers and beautify interest. Eating everyday food also can help to save you overeating or binging.

6. Avoid synthetic sweeteners: Artificial sweeteners had been related to hyperactivity and impulsivity in a few human beings, so it's miles crucial to avoid them.

7. Get masses of sleep: Getting enough sleep can help to enhance concentration, awareness, and strength levels for the duration of the day. It is important to try to get 7-nine hours of sleep each night time.

eight. Drink hundreds of water: Staying hydrated is essential for common health and can assist to decorate awareness and reputation.It's important to devour eight glasses of water or greater every day.

9. Exercise regularly: Regular exercising can help to beautify mood, lessen strain, and beautify attention. It's vital to workout for as a minimum half of an hour each day.

30 healthful meals for older women with ADHD

1. Baked Sweet Potato and Broccoli Frittata

2. Slow Cooker Vegetable Soup

3. Avocado Toast with Sun-Dried Tomatoes

four. Zucchini Noodles with Pesto and Tomatoes

5. Roasted Butternut Squash with Sage and Pine Nuts

6. Quinoa and Black Bean Stuffed Peppers

7. Salmon and Asparagus with Lemon-Dill Sauce

8. Sweet Potato and Kale Hash with Eggs

nine. Grilled Vegetable and Hummus Sandwich

10. Greek Yogurt Parfait with Fresh Fruit

eleven. Turkey and Quinoa Stuffed Peppers

12. Cauliflower Rice Burrito Bowl

thirteen. Quinoa and Avocado Salad

14. Skinny Baked Ziti

15. Peach and Avocado Salsa with Baked Tortilla Chips

16. Baked Egg Cups with Spinach and Feta

17. Stuffed Mushrooms with Walnuts and Feta

18. Lentil and Roasted Vegetable Salad

19. Roasted Tomato and Red Pepper Soup

20. Lentil and Sweet Potato Curry

21. Cucumber and Avocado Salad with Lime Vinaigrette

22. Overnight Oats with Fresh Fruit and Seeds

23. Vegetable Stir-Fry over Brown Rice

24. Chickpea and Spinach Curry

25. Lentil and Kale Soup

26. Quinoa and Roasted Vegetable Salad

27. Baked Salmon with Herbed Yogurt Sauce

28. Grilled Veggie and Feta Wrap

29. Tuna Salad with Avocado and Tomato

30. White Bean and Arugula Salad

Time Management as a method to control ADHD Symptoms in older girls

Time control is an effective method for dealing with ADHD signs in older women. It can assist them stay organized, stay on undertaking, and keep away from procrastination. Time manage can help older ladies stay on path with their goals and commitments and manipulate the impulsivity and distractibility this is regularly associated with ADHD.

Some strategies for time manipulate include:

1. Scheduling: Setting apart specific times for duties and sports sports can assist older ladies with ADHD stay on course and prepared. It can also help them prioritize obligations and ensure they'll be finishing critical obligations first.

2. Breaking down obligations: Breaking down responsibilities into smaller, greater manageable chunks can help older women with ADHD live centered and avoid turning into beaten with the useful resource of the mission handy.

three. Setting reminders: Using reminders together with alarms, sticky notes, or perhaps smartphone reminders can assist older women with ADHD stay organized and on assignment.

four. Prioritizing: Prioritizing obligations in step with significance can assist older women with ADHD live on course with their desires and commitments.

five. Taking breaks: Taking everyday breaks at some level inside the day can help older women with ADHD stay focused and avoid burnout.

6. Using a planner: Writing down obligations and time limits in a planner can help older women with ADHD undergo in mind vital facts and live organized.

7.Limiting distractions: Limiting distractions which includes television, social media, and get in touch with calls can help older women with ADHD stay targeted on their tasks.

8. Avoiding multitasking: Multitasking can be hard for older women with ADHD and

can motive confusion and disorganization. It is crucial to recognition on one mission at a time.

nine. Getting enough sleep: Sleep is important for cognitive functioning and staying prepared. Older women with ADHD ought to aim to get 7-eight hours of sleep steady with night time.

10. Seeking assist: If time management strategies aren't enough, older women with ADHD need to do not forget searching for expert help from a psychologist or psychiatrist.

By utilising time manipulate strategies, older ladies with ADHD can better manipulate their symptoms and lead a fulfillment lives.

Organization as a method for Managing ADHD Symptoms in older girls

1. Establish a Consistent Routine: Establishing a normal recurring can help older women with ADHD control their signs

through supplying shape and predictability. This can also additionally embody setting ordinary times for meals, exercise, sleep, and sports activities.

2. Break Tasks into Smaller Steps: Breaking down responsibilities into smaller, greater practicable steps can assist older girls with ADHD live targeted and prepared.

three. Use a Calendar: A calendar may be used to help girls stay organized and on the right tune with their each day duties. Setting reminders for crucial conferences, appointments, or responsibilities may be useful.

four. Simplify Multi-Step Processes: Simplifying multi-step procedures can assist older ladies with ADHD stay organized and on path. For example, breaking down the manner of getting prepared for art work into smaller steps can help ladies with ADHD live organized.

five. Take Breaks: Taking ordinary breaks at some level within the day can assist older girls with ADHD recharge and refocus. This might also embody taking time for physical hobby, rest, or mindfulness.

6. Use Technology to Stay Organized: Technology can be used to assist older women with ADHD stay organized. This can also include the use of a virtual calendar, reminders, or venture manage apps to help maintain music of important obligations and activities.

7. Develop Positive Self-Talk: Developing great self-communicate can help older women with ADHD live organized and on direction. This may additionally encompass high exceptional affirmations and galvanizing mind to help hold ladies prompted and centered.

eight. Prioritize Tasks: Prioritizing responsibilities can assist older girls with ADHD live prepared and heading within the proper path with their every day obligations. This may also additionally additionally consist of specializing in one challenge at a time and putting sensible dreams.

9. Seek Social Support: Seeking social useful resource may be beneficial for older ladies with ADHD. This may additionally embody speaking to own family, buddies, or a highbrow health expert approximately symptoms, traumatic conditions, and strategies for coping with ADHD.

10. Practice Mindfulness: Practicing mindfulness can assist ladies manipulate their ADHD signs by manner of supporting them live gift within the 2nd and focused on their obligations. This can also embody yoga, breathing physical activities, or meditation.

Delegation as a approach to govern ADHD Symptoms in older girls

Delegation is an effective approach to control ADHD signs and symptoms in older ladies. By delegating obligations which might be too overwhelming or hard to manipulate, an older lady can consciousness her power on the duties that she is capable of deal with and manipulate. Delegation also allows her to outsource responsibilities that she reveals hard or time-eating, which include managing her price variety or organizing her home. This can assist her to live organized and on challenge, even as also freeing up her energy to interest on obligations that she is better suitable to cope with. Additionally, delegation may be beneficial in offering shape to her day and supporting her to stay on course collectively along with her dreams. This may be mainly beneficial for older women with ADHD, who may additionally battle with impulsivity or loss of recognition. Delegation can also offer her with the assist she wants to manipulate her symptoms and signs and symptoms and signs. By having a person to help her stay prepared and at the right track, she may be capable of gain the shape and useful resource she desires to successfully manipulate her ADHD signs.

Delegation can also help to reduce pressure and tension levels related to ADHD symptoms and signs and signs in older ladies. By having someone to help manage duties which can be too overwhelming or time ingesting, it is able to help to lessen the emotions of overwhelm that frequently accompany ADHD. Additionally, having a person to help her stay on course and installation her day can assist to relieve a number of the pressure associated with managing her signs and symptoms and signs and symptoms and symptoms and signs and symptoms. Finally, delegation can be a precious tool in assisting older ladies with ADHD to maintain stability of their lives.

Chapter 4: Living With Adhd

Creating a Support System as approach of living with ADHD in older ladies

Creating a resource system is one of the maximum vital matters a lady with ADHD can do to control her condition. A strong assist machine facilitates to maintain a female centered, organized, and prompted. It additionally facilitates to decrease feelings of isolation and loneliness.

The first step in developing a aid system is to understand people who are invested in the lady's well-being. These also can embody circle of relatives individuals, buddies, co-humans, buddies, or on-line help organizations. It is essential to bear in mind that no longer all of these people want to be without delay worried in dealing with the woman's ADHD; they can offer emotional guide, encouragement, and recommendation.

Once the woman has diagnosed her manual system, it is vital to speak overtly and definitely. This allows the female to present an explanation for her needs and to gather feedback and help. If the girl is uncomfortable discussing her ADHD along side her help community, she might be able to undergo in thoughts talking to a therapist or becoming a member of a beneficial useful resource business enterprise. When growing a help tool, it is also crucial to maintain in mind the woman's way of existence. This consists of her every day ordinary, eating regimen, and exercising behavior. Making small changes, along side breaking large duties into smaller ones, taking ordinary breaks, and scheduling breaks for the duration of the day, can assist the girl stay organized and targeted.

Creating a help device is vital for older ladies with ADHD. By taking the time to discover her aid network, communicate brazenly, and prioritize her non-public properly being, a female can create a stable and supportive environment that facilitates her manage her scenario. Creating a resource device is likewise important for making sure that a girl with ADHD gets the care and remedy she needs. This can embody attempting to find expert assist, which includes seeing a therapist, attending guide companies, or journeying a clinical medical doctor. It is also essential to keep in thoughts that remedy may be essential to manipulate ADHD. Women have to speak their alternatives with their healthcare agency to find out the best treatment plan for their individual goals.

Finally, the female ought to make sure to take time for herself. Making time for relaxation and enjoyment sports sports can help reduce strain and anxiety. This may be as smooth as taking a stroll or reading a e-book.

Finding the Right Professional Help as way of residing with ADHD in older girls

Living with ADHD as an older lady may be hard and overwhelming. Finding the proper professional help may be a key issue in correctly coping with ADHD symptoms and symptoms. It's essential to discover a expert who is familiar with ADHD, and may offer the proper shape of help. You should look for a person with enjoy in on foot with adults with ADHD, in addition to an outstanding understanding of the annoying conditions adults face.

It's furthermore important to discover a person who's inclined to artwork with you to increase an individualized remedy plan. This plan need to encompass techniques for coping with symptoms and symptoms, as well as strategies for boosting functioning.

When seeking out expert assist, it's important to ask questions about the corporation's qualifications, experience, and method. You need to moreover inquire about the splendid forms of treatment they provide and the manner they can help you.

When seeking out professional assist, it's additionally important to undergo in thoughts the rate. Many specialists offer sliding scale expenses, making remedy greater cheap. Additionally, you will be able to discover low-fee or loose assets in your network.

The maximum crucial detail is to discover someone you revel in comfortable with. A suitable expert ought to be a person you can get hold of as actual with and communicate to overtly. Ultimately, finding the proper expert help need to make a massive difference in supporting you control your ADHD symptoms and symptoms and symptoms and signs and symptoms. Once you've decided the proper expert help, it's vital to live steady with remedy. This method attending all appointments and following via on any recommendations or techniques your agency indicates. It's moreover essential to hold in thoughts that remedy for ADHD is a manner. It may additionally take time to discover the right strategies, and it's crucial to be affected person and records. Additionally, you can want to modify your techniques as your signs and symptoms evolve. Many adults with ADHD have placed success in managing their signs and symptoms and signs and symptoms. With the right professional help and aid, you can find out the gear and property to efficaciously control your ADHD.

Finding Balance in Life for older ladies with ADHD

As an older lady with ADHD, locating balance in existence may be hard. It is vital to boom strategies to help control the symptoms of ADHD and to find out strategies to maintain your existence in stability. First, it is critical to recognize that your ADHD is part of who you are and it's miles critical to simply accept it. This will permit you to to understand your strengths and weaknesses, and to growth strategies that will help you to attain success. Second, it's far essential to create carrying sports and shape in your day. This can help to restriction distractions and help you stay targeted at the responsibilities at hand. This may also furthermore embody setting aside unique times to finish responsibilities and breaking massive duties into smaller, potential chunks.

Third, it's far crucial to create healthful conduct. This encompass retaining a healthful diet, getting sufficient sleep, and running out frequently. This can assist to beautify your physical and intellectual fitness, and assist you to stay targeted and prepared.

Fourth, it's far important to discover time for your self. This can contain such things as going for a walk, analyzing, or listening to music. This can help to lessen strain and allow for time to way thoughts and emotions. Finally, it's miles crucial to reach out for assist at the same time as wanted. This can consist of searching for expert assist from a therapist or a psychiatrist, or becoming a member of a help business enterprise for human beings with ADHD. It is critical to realize which you are not by myself and that assistance is available.

In addition to those techniques, it's far crucial to stay related with pals and own family. Making time for meaningful relationships can assist to lessen stress and provide emotional guide. It is likewise crucial to workout self-compassion. It is easy to turn out to be crushed and discouraged on the identical time as coping with your ADHD, but it is crucial to be kind and know-how to yourself. Finally, it is critical to take time to interest for your passions and interests. This can help to provide a experience of purpose and delight. Developing pastimes or taking lessons can assist to stimulate your thoughts and hold you engaged.

Chapter 5: Understanding Adhd And Anxiety

Attention Deficit Hyperactivity Disorder (ADHD) and tension are hard intellectual fitness conditions that, on the same time as professional collectively, can appreciably impact a female's existence. This bankruptcy serves as the muse for our exploration into those complex troubles, presenting an in-depth expertise of ADHD in girls, a higher examination of hysteria, and an exploration of the intersection among the 2.

Introduction to ADHD in Women

ADHD is typically related to hyperactivity and impulsivity, tendencies which are probably extra pretty without a doubt discovered in person men. However, the presentation of ADHD in ladies frequently differs, manifesting in subtler techniques that may be unnoticed or misinterpreted. This segment seeks to light up the right additives of ADHD in ladies, aiming to dispel misconceptions and lift recognition about the numerous ways this example can have an impact on humans.

Women with ADHD can also face tremendous annoying situations, inclusive of problems with hobby, business enterprise, and emotional law. These demanding situations, on the same time as present, might not conform to conventional expectancies of hyperactivity. The surrender result is an under diagnosis or misdiagnosis of ADHD in ladies, major to not on time intervention and help. By exploring the nuances of the manner ADHD gives in women, we empower readers to apprehend those patterns and endorse for proper identity.

Understanding the interplay among gender and ADHD is critical. Women might also extend coping mechanisms that masks their signs, which include perfectionism or people-attractive behaviors. These coping techniques can save you the recognition of underlying ADHD, perpetuating a cycle of frustration and self-doubt. Through actual-life reminiscences and case studies, we goal to offer relatable examples that resonate with the reviews of ladies who navigate life with ADHD, fostering a sense of connection and understanding.

Unpacking Anxiety: A Closer Look

Anxiety, a common associate to ADHD, presents some other layer of complexity to the worrying situations people face. This subchapter takes a deep dive into the multifaceted nature of hysteria, acknowledging that it is able to take place in numerous office work and intensities. For girls with ADHD, anxiety can be every a final results of the demanding conditions they face and a standalone condition that exacerbates their customary highbrow health.

Understanding anxiety requires a nuanced exploration of its manifestations. From generalized tension to precise phobias, panic troubles, and social tension, ladies with ADHD may enjoy a spectrum of hysteria-associated troubles. By examining those manifestations and supplying real-existence examples, we purpose to equip readers with the apprehend-a way to understand tension in its diverse paperwork.

Furthermore, the relationship among ADHD and tension is bidirectional. ADHD-related problems, alongside side government feature deficits and impulsivity, can make a contribution to heightened strain and tension. Conversely, continual anxiety can impair interest and interest, amplifying ADHD signs and symptoms and symptoms and symptoms. This reciprocal courting underscores the importance of addressing every conditions concurrently for effective intervention.

The Intersection of ADHD and Anxiety

The intersection of ADHD and anxiety creates a completely particular set of worrying conditions for women. This phase explores the dynamic interplay the various ones conditions, dropping slight on why they often coexist. Biological, highbrow, and social elements make a contribution to the tough relationship amongst ADHD and tension, making it crucial to adopt a comprehensive approach to intervention.

Biologically, both ADHD and tension are associated with changes in neurotransmitter hobby and thoughts function. Understanding these shared neurobiological mechanisms gives insights into why those situations often upward thrust up collectively. Psychologically, the regular disturbing conditions posed by means of using ADHD, consisting of difficulties with cognizance and enterprise enterprise, can make contributions to continual strain and anxiety. Socially, the stigma and misconceptions surrounding ADHD may additionally furthermore in addition exacerbate emotions of anxiety, developing a complicated net of interconnected reviews.

Recognizing the intersection of ADHD and anxiety is a vital step in the direction of holistic intervention. By addressing each conditions simultaneously, human beings can enjoy greater complete and sustainable improvements in their mental well-being. This bankruptcy units the degree for the realistic techniques and abilties added in next chapters, providing a basis of expertise that empowers women with ADHD and tension on their adventure toward resilience and recuperation.

Foundations of Dialectical Behavior Therapy (DBT)

Dialectical Behavior Therapy (DBT) gives a whole framework for people struggling with emotional dysregulation, a common mission for ladies with ADHD and anxiety. This bankruptcy lays the idea for know-how and utilising DBT ideas, emphasizing their relevance and effectiveness in addressing the right goals of this demographic.

Overview of DBT Principles

DBT, superior through the use of the use of Dr. Marsha M. Linehan, integrates cognitive-behavioral strategies with ideas of mindfulness and recognition. This subchapter gives an extensive evaluation of the foundational principles of DBT, outlining the 4 important modules: Mindfulness, Distress Tolerance, Emotional Regulation, and Interpersonal Effectiveness. Each module is designed to equip humans with competencies to navigate emotional demanding situations, alter intense emotions, and improve interpersonal relationships.

Central to DBT is the concept of dialectics, emphasizing the synthesis of seemingly opposing ideas. This method encourages recognition and change simultaneously, fostering a balanced attitude on one's opinions. The incorporation of dialectics allows ladies with ADHD and anxiety to validate their feelings at the same time as on foot in the route of behavioral adjustments, promoting a revel in of empowerment and self-efficacy.

DBT furthermore emphasizes the significance of a therapist-patron collaboration, developing a dynamic in which both activities paintings inside the path of the patron's desires. The subchapter explores the therapist's function in validating the consumer's tales on the same time as encouraging willpower to change. By organising a recovery alliance grounded in recognition and information, DBT lays the foundation for significant improvement.

Mindfulness Skills for Women with ADHD

Mindfulness is a cornerstone of DBT, and its software program is mainly useful for women with ADHD. This phase explores mindfulness as a effective device for handling attention troubles and emotional dysregulation. Mindfulness includes cultivating present-2d attention with out judgment, permitting human beings to study their thoughts and emotions with out turning into crushed.

For women with ADHD, working closer to mindfulness can enhance attention and recognition. Mindfulness skills which incorporates focused interest and non-judgmental hobby provide precious device to navigate the annoying situations of distractibility. This subchapter introduces sensible mindfulness sporting activities tailor-made to the right dreams of girls with ADHD, fostering a deeper know-how of their mind and feelings.

Mindfulness additionally plays a essential feature in emotion regulation. By growing the potential to have a look at and describe feelings without judgment, women with

ADHD can gain greater control over immoderate emotional responses. Mindfulness techniques, which consist of aware respiratory and frame test physical sports, are explored as powerful strategies for cultivating emotional cognizance and fostering a more revel in of calm.

Chapter 6: Emotional Regulation Strategies

Emotional law is a applicable detail of nicely-being, and for girls grappling with ADHD and anxiety, getting to know powerful techniques is essential. This economic destroy delves into the difficult method of understanding and dealing with emotions, imparting insights into figuring out and naming feelings, the use of DBT talents for emotional expression, and developing a customized emotional law toolkit.

Identifying and Naming Emotions

For many girls with ADHD and tension, the revel in of feelings can be excessive and overwhelming. This phase specializes within the foundational step of identifying and naming emotions, a crucial ability in the emotional law approach. Understanding emotions is like deciphering a complex language; it calls for self-interest and the capability to distinguish amongst one in every of a kind emotional states.

The monetary catastrophe explores the nuances of emotional identity, emphasizing the significance of recognizing each primary and secondary feelings. Primary emotions are the straight away reactions to a scenario, on the equal time as secondary feelings are layered responses that often mask the number one ones. By delving into case studies and sensible examples, girls with ADHD and tension can gain a deeper expertise in their emotional landscape.

DBT encourages using emotion law worksheets to facilitate the way of identifying and naming feelings. These worksheets offer a established framework for human beings to pinpoint their feelings, find out their triggers, and track patterns through the years. By learning the capability of figuring out and naming feelings, women with ADHD and anxiety can advantage more clarity approximately their inner stories, laying the foundation for effective emotional regulation.

DBT Skills for Emotional Expression

Once emotions are diagnosed, the subsequent step is expressing them in healthful and nice techniques. This section introduces DBT competencies for emotional expression, emphasizing the significance of communication and self-expression. For ladies with ADHD and anxiety, expressing emotions can be difficult, given the depth in their emotions and capacity troubles in verbalizing their studies.

The financial ruin explores the DBT skills of "DEAR MAN," an acronym representing Describe, Express, Assert, Reinforce, Mindful, Appear confident, and Negotiate. This skills offers a dependent technique to assertiveness and powerful conversation, empowering ladies to express their wishes and feelings assertively while keeping self-apprehend and interest for others.

Additionally, the usage of modern stores along side journaling, art, or track is delivered as precious gear for emotional expression. These sports provide opportunity strategies to supply complex feelings, imparting a manner of self-discovery and catharsis. By incorporating a variety of expressive techniques, ladies with ADHD and tension can diversify their emotional toolbox, enhancing their functionality to navigate and speak their inner evaluations.

Creating an Emotional Regulation Toolkit

Building at the capabilities of figuring out and expressing feelings, this segment guides girls in developing a customised emotional regulation toolkit. Recognizing that no longer all techniques paintings universally, the economic break encourages humans to curate a set of strategies that resonate with their specific desires and options.

The toolkit encompasses an entire lot of proof-based totally certainly strategies, along with mindfulness physical activities, grounding strategies, and sensory modulation sports. Mindfulness, as added in Chapter 2, continues to play a pivotal function in emotional regulation, fostering a non-judgmental popularity of the triumphing 2d. Grounding strategies, together with the five-four-three-2-1 approach, offer sensory anchors that assist anchor people at some stage in moments of emotional turbulence.

Furthermore, the economic smash explores the benefits of creating a bodily toolkit, at the aspect of assembling a fixed of comforting gadgets or developing a chosen space for relaxation. This tangible detail of the toolkit serves as a tangible reminder of the character's determination to emotional properly-being.

Incorporating self-compassion practices, the toolkit encourages women with ADHD and tension to deal with themselves with kindness and information within the direction of tough emotional moments. This phase gives sensible guidance on growing a self-compassion mindset, emphasizing the importance of embracing imperfections and learning from reviews.

By combining those elements right into a whole emotional law toolkit, ladies with ADHD and tension gain a flexible beneficial useful resource to navigate the complexities in their emotional landscape. This customized toolkit not best complements emotional well-being but additionally empowers people to take an lively function of their intellectual fitness adventure, fostering resilience and flexibility inside the face of emotional traumatic situations.

Interpersonal Effectiveness in Women with ADHD

Interpersonal effectiveness is a critical aspect of navigating the complex panorama of relationships, and for ladies coping with ADHD, this ability will become even more essential. This economic smash makes a speciality of the unique worrying conditions that girls with ADHD may furthermore encounter in their relationships, exploring techniques for navigating the ones demanding situations, developing assertiveness competencies to address tension, and putting in powerful barriers to speak needs.

Navigating Relationships with ADHD Challenges

Women with ADHD regularly face extremely good challenges of their interpersonal relationships, beginning from issues with interest and organisation to struggles with impulse control. This segment delves into the nuanced components of navigating relationships while managing ADHD, recognizing that these annoying situations can impact numerous dynamics, from non-public friendships to romantic partnerships.

Acknowledging the significance of self-attention in recognizing how ADHD may additionally show up in social interactions. By know-how one's unique ADHD-associated traits and potential impact on relationships, women can take proactive steps to cope with disturbing situations and leverage their strengths. Case research and real-life examples provide relatable eventualities, providing insights into how ADHD can also additionally effect verbal exchange styles, time manage, and emotional regulation inner relationships.

The segment explores the position of schooling and open verbal exchange in fostering know-how amongst pals, circle of relatives, and companions. By sharing insights about ADHD, ladies can create an surroundings wherein their loved ones recognize the nuances of the scenario, principal to extended empathy and collaborative hassle-fixing. The bankruptcy emphasizes the importance of mutual manual in constructing resilient relationships that accommodate the traumatic situations related to ADHD.

Assertiveness Skills for Women with Anxiety

Assertiveness is a vital interpersonal potential that ladies with ADHD and tension often discover difficult to recognize. This subchapter focuses on growing assertiveness capabilities tailor-made to the particular dreams of women dealing with every ADHD and tension. Assertiveness entails expressing one's desires and reviews at the same time as respecting the rights and limitations of others.

Women with ADHD can also additionally encounter tension almost about preserving themselves, fearing judgment or battle. The financial ruin introduces sensible techniques, which include the DESC script (Describe, Express, Specify, Consequences), to manual assertive communique. This based approach assists ladies in articulating their thoughts and desires honestly, reducing tension associated with potential misunderstandings.

Cognitive restructuring, a key issue of DBT, is also added as a device for handling stressful thoughts associated with assertiveness. By hard and reframing horrible ideals approximately expressing goals, women can assemble self assurance of their capability to assert themselves efficaciously. Role-playing carrying events and real-international examples offer concrete packages of assertiveness capabilities, empowering ladies to navigate interpersonal interactions with advanced self-guarantee.

Setting Boundaries and Communicating Needs

Setting boundaries is vital for preserving wholesome relationships, and this section addresses the significance of setting up smooth boundaries for girls with ADHD. The monetary ruin explores how ADHD-related annoying situations, together with impulsivity and hassle with time manage, can effect the potential to set and maintain limitations. Practical strategies are added to help girls find out their desires, talk limits efficiently, and navigate situations wherein boundaries can be tested.

The characteristic of mindfulness in boundary placing, encouraging women to stay attuned to their very non-public goals and understand whilst boundaries may moreover need adjustment. Additionally, assertiveness abilties from the previous phase are reinforced as treasured machine for communicating and reinforcing limitations in severa social contexts.

Effective boundary putting is intently related to self-advocacy, and the economic wreck gives steerage on how ladies with ADHD can advise for his or her desires in each personal and expert settings. By cultivating a proactive technique to verbal exchange, girls can foster a supportive environment that respects their boundaries at the identical time as selling information amongst friends, colleagues, and loved ones.

Overall, this financial disaster serves as a complete guide for girls with ADHD seeking out to decorate their interpersonal effectiveness. By navigating relationships with ADHD demanding situations, growing assertiveness abilities to cope with anxiety, and putting barriers to talk desires, women can assemble stronger, greater resilient connections that manual their well-being and personal increase.

Chapter 7: Walking The Middle Path

Walking the center route is a essential idea in Dialectical Behavior Therapy (DBT), and this financial ruin explores its software program application within the context of ADHD and tension. Finding balance amid opposing forces becomes important for women navigating the ones conditions, and the subchapters delve into balancing opposites, locating middle floor in annoying conditions, and embracing dialectics for number one intellectual well-being.

Balancing Opposites within the Context of ADHD

ADHD frequently offers worrying situations that include balancing opposing forces, together with the need for form in preference to the desire for spontaneity, or the anxiety among hyperfocus and distractibility. This segment delves into the artwork of balancing opposites in the context of ADHD, spotting that extremes may be counterproductive.

The chapter starts through exploring the dichotomy of form and flexibility. While people with ADHD might also moreover crave shape for company and consciousness, rigid workouts can come to be stifling. Striking a balance involves developing bendy systems that offer a framework with out sacrificing adaptability. Practical techniques for time control, which include the use of seen schedules and breaking duties into smaller, possible steps, are delivered to help women with ADHD discover the equilibrium among structure and versatility.

Another issue of balancing opposites is managing the interplay between hyperfocus and distractibility. Women with ADHD may additionally experience durations of extreme recognition, called hyperfocus, but war with distractibility ultimately of a whole lot a great deal less appealing duties. The financial ruin gives insights into leveraging hyperfocus for productivity on the equal time as enforcing strategies to mitigate distractions finally of much much less stimulating sports.

Recognizing the want for every is crucial for intellectual properly-being. Strategies for powerful social engagement, which include placing realistic expectations and speakme desires, are cited along the importance of carving out moments for solitude to recharge.

Finding Middle Ground in Anxious Situations

Anxiety can create severe perceptions of conditions, primary to black-and-white wondering and a experience of urgency. This subchapter makes a speciality of finding the center ground in stressful conditions, promoting a greater balanced attitude that mitigates the impact of tension on decision-making and emotional properly-being.

The financial disaster introduces the ability of "Wise Mind," a idea essential to DBT that includes finding the intersection among rational questioning and emotional revel in. This capacity encourages girls with ADHD and anxiety to technique conditions with every reason and emotion, fostering a more nuanced knowledge and response.

Practical techniques, collectively with mindfulness and grounding sporting activities, are explored as gear to anchor oneself in the gift 2d throughout irritating episodes. By cultivating popularity and staying grounded, women can better navigate worrying conditions with out succumbing to impulsive reactions or catastrophic wondering.

Additionally, the phase addresses the significance of self-compassion in stressful moments. Women are guided to famend their feelings with out judgment and address themselves with kindness. This self-compassionate technique serves as a powerful antidote to the horrible self-talk that regularly accompanies tension, selling emotional resilience and well-being.

Embracing Dialectics for Mental Well-being

The concept of dialectics, vital to DBT, consists of recognizing and reconciling opposites. In the context of highbrow well-being, embracing dialectics is ready acknowledging the coexistence of conflicting mind and emotions, and locating a synthesis that fosters stability and growth.

Encourages women to include the dialectic of popularity and trade. Rather than viewing these as opposing forces, they'll be seen as complementary. This includes accepting the fact of the winning 2d at the identical time as actively operating closer to remarkable adjustments. Practical techniques for integrating popularity and trade, together with the use of the information of "Radical Acceptance," are delivered to empower ladies with ADHD and anxiety to navigate worrying conditions with resilience.

Women with ADHD and tension can also moreover understand vulnerability as a weakness, however acknowledging and expressing vulnerability can be a deliver of strength and connection. Strategies for cultivating emotional resilience, along with looking for guide and reframing vulnerability as courage, are said to empower girls in embracing the complete spectrum in their emotional evaluations.

Additionally, the dialectic of autonomy and interdependence is explored. Balancing independence with a healthy reliance on others is vital for intellectual nicely-being. This includes recognizing whilst to are attempting to find resource and while to mention autonomy. Strategies for powerful verbal exchange and collaboration, together with the DEAR MAN capacity introduced in Chapter four, contribute to locating this stability.

Walking the center route is a dynamic and ongoing approach. By embracing dialectics, women with ADHD and anxiety can navigate the complexities of their mental fitness

Chapter 8: Radical Acceptance In Daily Life

Radical reputation, a center principle of Dialectical Behavior Therapy (DBT), is a transformative potential that holds unique significance for human beings dealing with ADHD and anxiety. This financial ruin explores the software of radical recognition in every day existence, emphasizing the importance of embracing truth, letting pass of judgment and self-criticism, and applying radical recognition in tough moments.

Embracing Reality with ADHD and Anxiety

Living with ADHD and tension frequently consists of grappling with a fact that won't align with societal expectancies or personal aspirations. This phase delves into the concept of embracing reality, acknowledging the precise traumatic situations and strengths that encompass ADHD and tension. Radical elegance consists of absolutely acknowledging and validating one's present events without judgment, fostering a revel in of inner peace and resilience.

Addressing the societal narratives and stigmas surrounding ADHD and tension. Women frequently face out of doors judgments or internalized beliefs about their capabilities and well worth. Radical reputation encourages letting drift of societal expectations and embracing the reality of individual critiques. Practical bodily sports, together with mindfulness strategies and self-reflected photo prompts, are delivered to help girls domesticate a non-judgmental cognizance in their mind and feelings.

The reputation of boundaries and imperfections. Women with ADHD can also come across demanding conditions associated with government competencies, time manage, and organizational talents. Radical splendor includes acknowledging those boundaries without self-blame and exploring sensible techniques to paintings inside the ones constraints. By embracing reality, women can increase a compassionate facts in their particular strengths and demanding situations, paving the manner for correct self-expression.

Letting Go of Judgment and Self-Criticism

The relentless cycle of judgment and self-criticism is a commonplace conflict for human beings with ADHD and anxiety. This subchapter delves into the transformative electricity of letting pass of judgment and self-grievance through the lens of radical reputation. This skills consists of recognizing and tough poor mind, cultivating self-compassion, and fostering a extra high-quality courting with oneself.

The position of mindfulness in breaking the cycle of judgment and self-grievance. Mindfulness techniques, together with ob.Serving thoughts without attachment and working towards self-compassionate meditation, function gear to break awful idea patterns. By developing focus of the inner speak, girls can begin to venture computerized judgments and update self-vital mind with more compassionate and balanced perspectives.

The idea of Wise Mind, brought in previous chapters, is revisited as a guiding precept for letting cross of self-criticism. Wise Mind includes locating the intersection amongst rational questioning and emotional experience, permitting women to technique self-reflected photo with a balanced and compassionate mind-set. Practical bodily sports, which incorporates journaling turns on and self-affirmations, are provided to beneficial aid the cultivation of self-compassion and the release of self-critical judgments.

The societal misconceptions surrounding ADHD and tension can make contributions to a awful self-picture. Radical popularity includes difficult those out of doors judgments, recognizing their invalidity, and growing a experience of self esteem unbiased of societal expectations. By letting cross of external judgments and embracing self-attractiveness, women can foster a pleasant and empowering self-narrative.

Applying Radical Acceptance in Challenging Moments

Challenging moments, whether or now not or now not associated with ADHD or tension, are an inevitable part of existence. This section focuses on the sensible software of radical reputation in navigating tough situations. Radical reputation entails acknowledging and completely experiencing tough moments with out resistance, fostering resilience and flexibility.

The idea of distress tolerance, a capacity introduced in in advance chapters. Distress tolerance strategies, collectively with the TIPP potential set (Temperature, Intense Exercise, Paced Breathing, and Paired Muscle Relaxation), are revisited as powerful tool for coping with extreme feelings in the moment. By utilising misery tolerance talents, women can navigate hard moments with extra ease and save you the escalation of emotional misery.

The segment moreover introduces the idea of finding this means that in tough conditions. Radical attractiveness entails recognizing the restrictions of manipulate and reframing hard moments as possibilities for growth and gaining knowledge of. Women are endorsed to discover the education inherent in tough situations, cultivating a attitude that promotes personal development and resilience.

Practical techniques for utilising radical reputation in tough moments include the talent of "Half-Smiling," a manner designed to shift the emotional revel in via adopting a mild and accepting facial expression. Additionally, the usage of tremendous affirmations and self-compassionate statements is brought as a manner of selling a extra great and accepting attitude in the course of difficult instances.

Moreover, the phase emphasizes the significance of network and help in tough moments. Seeking assist from cherished ones or intellectual health specialists can beautify the software of radical attractiveness via providing a network of expertise and encouragement. The bankruptcy gives steerage on effective verbal exchange and collaboration, reinforcing the rate of shared memories and mutual resource.

In end, the talent of radical popularity is a effective device for ladies dealing with ADHD and tension of their each day lives. By embracing truth, letting move of judgment and self-complaint, and utilising radical reputation in hard moments, women can cultivate a mind-set of resilience, self-compassion, and real residing. This financial disaster serves as a sensible guide for integrating radical popularity into every day practices, fostering a wonderful and empowering method to navigating the complexities of ADHD and anxiety.

Skill-Building for Time Management

Time control is a essential detail of each day life, and for human beings with ADHD, it could pose specific demanding situations. This monetary spoil makes a speciality of talent-building for powerful time control, addressing the precise difficulties related to ADHD and introducing DBT techniques to beautify organizational competencies. Additionally, the bankruptcy explores the connection among dependent carrying activities and tension bargain, presenting practical insights for developing a balanced and supportive day by day time table.

ADHD and the Challenge of Time

Individuals with ADHD often face excellent demanding situations nearly about dealing with time. Issues alongside side problems with hobby, enterprise, and impulsivity can significantly impact the potential to prioritize responsibilities and cling to schedules. This phase delves into the precise traumatic situations posed by way of manner of ADHD in the realm of time control, presenting insights into the underlying factors and their effect on each day existence.

The concept of time blindness, a phenomenon common in humans with ADHD. Time blindness entails a distorted perception of the passage of time, principal to problems estimating how prolonged responsibilities will take and the tendency to underestimate time commitments. By expertise the effect of time blindness, human beings can extend strategies to seize up in this venture, together with setting timers, using seen schedules, and breaking responsibilities into smaller, more capacity increments.

Executive abilties, in conjunction with making plans, prioritization, and impulse manipulate, are frequently impaired in people with ADHD. The chapter introduces sensible physical sports activities and cognitive strategies to enhance govt talents, empowering humans to higher navigate the complexities of time control.

The emotional detail of time manage is explored. Individuals with ADHD also can enjoy frustration, tension, or a sense of failure related to problems in handling time successfully. The monetary damage emphasizes the significance of cultivating a pleasant mind-set, reframing setbacks as possibilities for mastering, and incorporating self-compassion into the method of developing time management abilties.

DBT Strategies for Effective Time Management

Dialectical Behavior Therapy (DBT) offers some of strategies that can be specifically useful for humans with ADHD searching for to beautify their time control competencies. This segment introduces DBT strategies tailored to cope with an appropriate demanding situations associated with ADHD, presenting a based totally completely and entire approach to beautify organizational competencies.

The exercising of mindfulness consists of growing an objective interest of the present day-day 2d. For humans with ADHD, incorporating mindfulness strategies can decorate interest and attention, contributing to improved time management. Practical sports activities, including conscious respiration and grounding techniques, are delivered as equipment to promote mindfulness in every day sports sports.

The section moreover delves into the DBT expertise of "Check the Facts," which inspires human beings to objectively test out a scenario in advance than reacting. Applying this expertise to time control consists of evaluating expectancies, putting realistic desires, and spotting functionality boundaries. By incorporating "Check the Facts," human beings should make knowledgeable alternatives about the manner to allocate their time and energy effectively.

Moreover, the financial disaster introduces the competencies of "ABC PLEASE," emphasizing the importance of self-care in optimizing cognitive functioning. Adequate sleep, balanced nutrients, and everyday exercising contribute to normal nicely-being and may simply impact interest, awareness, and time control. Practical steerage on incorporating self-care into daily sporting activities is supplied, recognizing the interconnectedness of physical fitness and effective time manipulate.

The idea of "Opposite Action" is explored as a device to counteract procrastination and avoidance behaviors. Individuals with ADHD may additionally war with initiating responsibilities because of a fear of failure or overwhelm. "Opposite Action" consists of consciously deciding on behaviors which can be opposite to the emotional urges, fostering a experience of feat and momentum in time manipulate.

Creating a Structured Routine for Anxiety Reduction

Beyond the stressful situations posed via the usage of ADHD, anxiety can in addition complicate effective time control. This segment explores the intricate dating amongst established exercises and tension good buy, supplying sensible insights into the appearance of a day by day time table that promotes a revel in of order, predictability, and emotional properly-being.

Individuals with tension may also moreover moreover enjoy time as fleeting or distorted, contributing to a feel of urgency or time stress. Creating a primarily based routine acts as a grounding mechanism, supplying a easy framework for sports activities and reducing the effect of tension at the perception of time.

DBT skills of "Building Mastery" as a method to enhance self-efficacy and decrease anxiety related to time manipulate. "Building Mastery" consists of project sports activities that foster a revel in of fulfillment and competence. By incorporating mastery-constructing sports proper right into a installed ordinary, humans can decorate self assurance and decrease anxiety related to time-related challenges.

The benefits of making a visual agenda or planner. Visual tools offer a tangible illustration of time commitments, final dates, and priorities, aiding human beings in preserving a smooth assessment in their time table. Practical suggestions for designing and utilizing visible schedules are supplied, catering to the visible studying options frequently related to ADHD.

Moreover, the concept of "Behavioral Activation" is added as a method of preventing the lethargy and inertia which could accompany anxiety. Behavioral activation includes breaking duties into smaller, greater possible steps and regularly increasing interest tiers. By incorporating behavioral activation right right into a structured normal, people can triumph over the paralysis often associated with tension and assemble momentum in their time manipulate efforts.

By understanding the unique disturbing situations posed with the resource of the usage of ADHD, incorporating DBT strategies for powerful time manage, and developing a mounted habitual for anxiety discount, humans can extend sensible and sustainable techniques to coping with their time and fostering desired properly-being.

Coping with Overwhelm and Burnout

Coping with crush and burnout is a crucial detail of keeping intellectual nicely-being, in particular for girls dealing with ADHD. This bankruptcy explores the signs of weigh down, introduces Dialectical Behavior Therapy (DBT) practices for preventing burnout, and gives self-care strategies tailored to relieve anxiety. By addressing the ones elements, girls can domesticate resilience, navigate demanding conditions efficaciously, and prioritize their intellectual health.

Recognizing Signs of Overwhelm in Women with ADHD

Recognizing the signs and symptoms and symptoms of overwhelm is a crucial step in proactively handling one's highbrow fitness. For ladies with ADHD, weigh down can show up in numerous methods, from heightened stress tiers to a experience of paralysis within the face of multiple responsibilities. This segment of the monetary ruin explores the nuanced signs and symptoms of weigh down unique to women managing ADHD, presenting insights into the early signs and symptoms and signs and symptoms that could manual timely interventions.

Acknowledging the interconnectedness of ADHD-associated traumatic conditions and crush. The problem in coping with time, preserving attention, and handling sensory stimuli can make contributions to a heightened susceptibility to crush. Real-life conditions and case research offer relatable examples, helping girls in figuring out patterns and triggers associated with overwhelm in their very personal lives.

The emotional elements of crush, emphasizing the vicinity of heightened sensitivity and emotional reactivity. Women with ADHD also can revel in intense feelings in reaction to out of doors stimuli, contributing to a feel of being emotionally flooded. The economic ruin introduces sensible strategies, which includes emotional law strategies and grounding sports, to assist women navigate and modify their feelings ultimately of overwhelming moments.

Additionally, the phase highlights the cognitive elements of crush, collectively with demanding situations in choice-making and hassle-solving. Cognitive techniques, inclusive of breaking duties into smaller, extra doable steps and placing practical dreams, are delivered to guide girls in preserving cognitive readability and reducing the cognitive load contributing to overwhelm.

Preventing Burnout thru DBT Practices

Preventing burnout is a proactive method to keeping mental well-being, particularly for human beings managing ADHD. Dialectical Behavior Therapy (DBT) practices provide valuable system for preventing burnout thru fostering emotional regulation, interpersonal effectiveness, and self-attention. This phase delves into the application of DBT practices as a protection diploma in competition to burnout, spotting the particular demanding situations confronted thru women dealing with ADHD.

The DBT skills of "PLEASE MASTER," which emphasizes the importance of attending to physical nicely-being to optimize emotional resilience. Women with ADHD may be greater vulnerable to burnout because of the desires of managing ADHD-related stressful conditions. Practical steering on prioritizing adequate sleep, balanced vitamins, and everyday exercising is furnished, empowering girls to take proactive steps in preventing burnout.

The section introduces the concept of "Vulnerability Factors" inside the context of burnout prevention. Recognizing non-public vulnerabilities, which consist of the effect of stressors or environmental factors, is essential in searching ahead to and addressing potential burnout. The financial ruin publications girls in identifying their precise vulnerability factors and growing strategies to mitigate their effect on highbrow well-being.

The DBT talent of "Building Mastery" as a way of stopping burnout. Engaging in sports that foster a sense of achievement and competence can contribute to resilience and save you the depletion of emotional belongings. Practical sports activities sports and examples are provided to guide women in incorporating mastery-building sports into their every day workout exercises.

Women with ADHD may additionally battle with setting and retaining barriers because of demanding situations in impulse manage and assertiveness. DBT talents brought in in advance chapters, which includes the DEAR MAN capabilities for interpersonal effectiveness, are revisited to manual women in establishing and talking boundaries efficaciously, reducing the danger of burnout.

Self-Care Techniques for Anxiety Relief

Self-care is a cornerstone of highbrow fitness, and for ladies managing ADHD and anxiety, it turns into a crucial issue of tension remedy. This segment of the monetary catastrophe explores self-care techniques mainly tailored to alleviate tension, acknowledging the complicated courting amongst self-care practices and highbrow nicely-being.

The bankruptcy begins thru manner of analyzing the effect of tension on self-care, recognizing that heightened anxiety ranges can prevent the initiation and renovation of self-care workout routines. Practical strategies for breaking self-care into smaller, more achievable steps are delivered, permitting ladies to navigate anxiety and step by step embody self-care into their every day lives.

DBT expertise of "Wise Mind ACCEPTS," presenting a framework for self-soothing sports activities sports to alleviate tension. The financial disaster courses women in figuring out personalised self-soothing techniques, which includes mission thrilling sports activities activities, schooling deep respiratory, or growing a calming environment. These sports activities make contributions to emotional regulation and offer a toolkit for tension comfort.

Women with ADHD may be mainly sensitive to sensory stimuli, and the monetary catastrophe introduces realistic techniques, which consist of sensory grounding sports and developing sensory-fine areas, to promote a feel of calm and reduce anxiety.

Chapter 9: Goal Setting And Progress Tracking

Goal setting and development monitoring are pivotal components of private improvement, specifically for people handling ADHD. This bankruptcy delves into the art work of placing sensible dreams with problems for ADHD, introduces effective strategies for tracking improvement in anxiety management, and emphasizes the importance of celebrating successes alongside the Dialectical Behavior Therapy (DBT) adventure. By exploring those additives, human beings can cultivate a proactive technique to private increase, beautify their resilience, and foster a powerful mindset.

Setting Realistic Goals with ADHD Considerations

Setting realistic dreams is a nuanced method, and individuals with ADHD face particular challenges that can effect purpose success. This segment of the monetary damage delves into the intricacies of purpose setting with problems for ADHD, providing practical insights and strategies to beautify the danger of fulfillment.

The bankruptcy starts offevolved offevolved with the useful useful resource of addressing the impact of impulsivity on intention putting. Individuals with ADHD can be extra liable to placing impulsive and unrealistic desires, major to frustration and setbacks. Practical techniques, which encompass implementing a pause in advance than committing to a aim and breaking huge goals into smaller, greater doable steps, are delivered to mitigate the effect of impulsivity at the aim-putting technique.

Furthermore, the phase explores the area of executive talents in intention putting. Challenges in planning, commercial enterprise corporation, and time manage associated with ADHD can hinder the a achievement pursuit of goals. The financial ruin introduces cognitive strategies, inclusive of visualizing the motive, the use of out of doors reminders, and incorporating established physical activities, to help humans in navigating government characteristic annoying situations and enhancing purpose attainment.

Moreover, the section addresses the idea of goal flexibility. Individuals with ADHD may additionally moreover stumble upon surprising barriers or adjustments in situations that necessitate modifications to desires. Embracing flexibility includes spotting even as to evolve goals and celebrating development, even though it deviates from the particular plan. The financial disaster gives steerage on developing a attitude that values adaptability and resilience within the pursuit of desires.

Monitoring Progress in Anxiety Management

Monitoring improvement in tension management is crucial for humans navigating the complexities of hysteria, specifically within the context of ADHD. This segment of the bankruptcy explores effective strategies for tracking improvement in tension manage, providing realistic device to enhance self-recognition and refine coping mechanisms.

The financial disaster starts with the useful resource of emphasizing the significance of self-tracking. Developing self-consciousness consists of frequently assessing emotional states, triggers, and coping strategies related to anxiety. Practical wearing activities, such as mood monitoring and journaling, are delivered to empower humans to reveal their development, understand patterns, and make informed modifications to their tension manage strategies.

Furthermore, the phase explores the function of mindfulness in progress tracking.

Mindfulness techniques, which consist of body scans and recognition of breath, offer human beings with gadget to live present and test their emotional responses to anxiety. By incorporating mindfulness into development tracking, humans can increase a deeper records in their reactions and cultivate a conscious approach to tension control.

Moreover, the financial ruin introduces the concept of behavioral tracking. This includes monitoring behaviors associated with tension, together with avoidance or protection-looking for behaviors, and gradually introducing greater adaptive responses. Practical strategies for behavioral monitoring, consisting of the use of a conduct diary and putting small, feasible behavioral dreams, are furnished to guide people in cultivating fine behavioral styles in tension management.

Additionally, the phase addresses the importance of looking for external feedback.

Engaging in open verbal exchange with trusted human beings, together with highbrow health professionals or supportive friends, offers precious perspectives on development and capability areas for improvement. The financial ruin gives guidance on powerful communication and collaboration to beautify development monitoring through outside feedback.

Celebrating Successes alongside the DBT Journey

Celebrating successes is a essential issue of maintaining motivation and fostering a high-quality mind-set alongside the Dialectical Behavior Therapy (DBT) adventure. This segment of the financial ruin explores the significance of acknowledging achievements, every big and small, and offers realistic insights into incorporating birthday party as a ordinary workout in personal increase.

The monetary catastrophe starts offevolved with the useful resource of studying the concept of validation. Validation includes spotting and putting forward one's efforts and development. For people with ADHD and tension, validation turns into a effective device in cultivating a exceptional self-narrative. Practical wearing sports, which include self-affirmations and growing a success mag, are delivered to guide people in embracing validation as a daily exercising.

Furthermore, the phase explores the placement of self-compassion in celebrating successes. Individuals coping with ADHD and anxiety may also encounter setbacks and worrying conditions alongside their journey, making self-compassion a essential component of keeping resilience. The financial disaster gives strategies for integrating self-compassionate practices, together with self-kindness and mindfulness, into the birthday party of successes.

Moreover, the financial smash introduces the DBT expertise of "Accumulating Positive Emotions" as a technique for building a effective emotional economic group. Engaging in sports activities that elicit tremendous emotions, whether or not via hobbies, social connections, or self-care practices, contributes to an emotional reserve that can be drawn upon inside the path of hard instances. Practical steerage on incorporating top notch emotional studies into each day sporting activities is supplied.

Additionally, the segment emphasizes the price of social birthday party. Sharing successes with trusted people, whether or no longer buddies, family, or assist companies, enhances the texture of connection and reinforces exceptional achievements. The financial break gives insights into effective verbal exchange and collaboration to create a supportive social surroundings that celebrates successes alongside the DBT adventure.

In quit, this economic catastrophe serves as an entire manual for humans managing ADHD, providing insights into setting realistic goals with worries for ADHD, tracking progress in tension manipulate, and celebrating successes alongside the DBT journey. By incorporating those practices into their lives, individuals can foster a proactive technique to personal boom, enhance resilience, and hold a high extraordinary mind-set as they navigate the complexities of ADHD and tension.

Sustaining Growth and Navigating Challenges

Sustaining increase and navigating annoying conditions are lifelong endeavors, especially for people managing ADHD and anxiety. This bankruptcy explores the incorporation of Dialectical Behavior Therapy (DBT) into long-time period techniques, addresses setbacks and the art work of persevering, and highlights the importance of building a supportive network for endured nicely-being. By delving into these additives, human beings can cultivate resilience, adaptability, and a enjoy of connectedness as they traverse the ongoing adventure of private growth.

Incorporating DBT into Long-Term Strategies

Incorporating Dialectical Behavior Therapy (DBT) into prolonged-time period strategies is a foundational element for individuals looking for sustained boom. This phase of the bankruptcy explores the ideas of DBT as enduring equipment for dealing with ADHD and anxiety, providing insights into how these techniques can grow to be important additives of one's day by day life.

Mindfulness, as delivered in earlier chapters, includes cultivating reputation of the triumphing second with out judgment. The section explores the position of mindfulness in selling emotional regulation, decreasing impulsivity, and fostering a revel in of groundedness in individuals managing

ADHD. Practical bodily sports activities, on the facet of conscious breathing and frame scans, are revisited to guide people in incorporating mindfulness into their prolonged-time period strategies.

Distress tolerance, a essential DBT talent, includes navigating hard conditions without escalating feelings. The bankruptcy provides insights into how misery tolerance techniques, which encompass self-soothing and radical popularity, can function enduring tools for coping with tension in the face of lifestyles's uncertainties. Real-existence scenarios and case studies offer relatable examples, illustrating the realistic software of misery tolerance in lengthy-term well-being.

Individuals with ADHD and tension often experience immoderate and fluctuating emotions, making emotion regulation a critical thing of sustained increase. The financial ruin revisits DBT abilties for emotion law, together with identifying and naming feelings and growing an emotional regulation toolkit, presenting realistic guidance on incorporating those competencies into lengthy-time period strategies for emotional properly-being.

The significance of ongoing purpose placing as a method of keeping motivation and purpose. Setting realistic desires, as explored in previous chapters, becomes an iterative machine in prolonged-time period techniques. The financial disaster offers insights into adapting desires to changing times, embracing flexibility, and celebrating ongoing successes to gas persisted growth.

Addressing Setbacks and Persevering

Addressing setbacks and persevering are inherent challenges in any adventure of personal boom. This phase of the bankruptcy explores the art work of navigating setbacks, knowledge their functionality impact on human beings dealing with ADHD and tension, and fostering resilience to persevere no matter boundaries.

Setbacks can take severa bureaucracy, from problems in time manipulate to heightened anxiety episodes. The segment offers a compassionate mind-set on setbacks, emphasizing that they're possibilities for learning and growth in choice to signs and symptoms of failure. Practical strategies, collectively with reframing setbacks and training self-compassion, are added to guide humans in navigating setbacks with resilience.

Individuals managing ADHD may additionally moreover moreover stumble upon disturbing situations in intention success due to govt characteristic difficulties or surprising boundaries. The financial ruin offers insights into adapting dreams in reaction to setbacks, fostering a thoughts-set that views setbacks as detours in choice to roadblocks. The DBT potential of "Wise Mind ACCEPTS" is revisited, providing humans machine for emotional law and angle-taking in the course of hard moments.

Self-efficacy, the belief in a unmarried's capability to build up dreams, is a effective determinant of resilience. The economic catastrophe introduces strategies for building self-efficacy, which includes mastery-constructing sports activities activities and excellent self-communicate, to empower humans in navigating setbacks and preserving momentum in their personal growth adventure.

Building a community of depended on human beings, whether or now not friends, own family, or highbrow health professionals, offers a precious useful resource for encouragement and steerage. The financial ruin offers insights into effective verbal exchange and collaboration in searching out assist, emphasizing the interconnectedness of perseverance and community.

Building a Supportive Community for Continued Well-being

Building a supportive network is a cornerstone of persisted well-being for human beings dealing with ADHD and anxiety. This segment of the economic disaster explores the significance of cultivating a community of help, whether through private connections, help groups, or expert relationships, and highlights the characteristic of network in keeping boom.

For human beings coping with ADHD and anxiety, a supportive community gives emotional validation, understanding, and a enjoy of belonging. The phase offers realistic steerage on fostering social connections, in conjunction with powerful communication and boundary-putting, to build a community that complements preferred nicely-being.

Support businesses, whether or not in-individual or on-line, provide a area for human beings to percentage opinions, benefit insights, and acquire encouragement from others handling comparable annoying situations. The bankruptcy gives insights into finding and taking part in manual agencies tailor-made to the goals of humans managing ADHD and anxiety, fostering a experience of network and shared knowledge.

Mental health experts, along with therapists and counselors, play a important characteristic in providing guidance, equipment, and techniques for individuals handling ADHD and anxiety. The monetary disaster gives insights into powerful collaboration with mental health specialists, emphasizing the price of open conversation and shared purpose-setting to optimize the blessings of professional help.

Additionally, the segment addresses the reciprocal nature of community guide. Building a supportive network entails not handiest receiving useful aid but furthermore contributing to the nicely-being of others. The financial ruin introduces the idea of "Building Mastery" in the context of network involvement, encouraging people to interact in sports activities that contribute to the properly-being of the larger community, fostering a enjoy of cause and connection.

For people coping with ADHD and tension, exploring the incorporation of DBT into lengthy-time period techniques, addressing setbacks and persevering, and highlighting the significance of building a supportive network for continued well-being. By embracing those ideas, people can navigate the complexities of their adventure, foster resilience, and domesticate a sense of connectedness that sustains their boom in the face of demanding situations.

Chapter 10: Unveiling Adhd In Women

The Gender Dynamics of ADHD

ADHD creates a exquisite sample and manifests itself in pretty a few techniques in the colourful cloth of the human enjoy. It becomes clean as we take a look at extra about ADHD that its outcomes are not the equal for women and men. Let's go out on a quest to discover the subtleties that set ladies's tales with ADHD aside as we remedy the complex dance of gender circle of relative's participants in the vicinity.

We want to first admit that for a long time, the majority of the general public's perception of ADHD has been male-centric as a way to apprehend the gender dynamics across the ailment. Popular view has been ruled via the cliché of the impetuous, hyperactive extra youthful boy who bounces off the walls in a classroom. Nevertheless, the stories of innumerable ladies and women who're coping with ADHD of their personal, regularly a good buy a great deal less obvious techniques have been eclipsed via this distorted depiction.

The problems and signs and symptoms and signs and symptoms and signs and symptoms of ADHD in girls can be greater subdued, ensuing in a complicated image that could defy conventional notions. Girls with ADHD normally pass undiagnosed, but boys with the disorder are frequently identified in youth primarily based mostly on overt symptoms and symptoms. Instead of disruptive behavior, their challenges can seem as inattentiveness, disorganization, or having a pipe dream.

Imagine an inquisitive and creative more youthful pupil who regularly loses her assignments and daydreams within the route of elegance. Her problems can be written off as smooth inattention or misinterpreted as a sign of laziness, which may result in an untreated prognosis of ADHD. This hypothetical state of affairs demonstrates the sensitive nature of ADHD in ladies, who regularly should negotiate a society that might not truly realise the nuances in their neurodivergent mentalities.

As young women become ladies, ADHD may also additionally furthermore have a more significant effect. The issues associated with ADHD can be made worse thru man or woman duties, together with walking a domestic and having a profession. Women may also moreover war with government feature troubles together with time manipulate and undertaking agency agency, which can be specifically difficult in a life-style that regularly demands best multitasking.

The propensity for girls with ADHD to internalize their demanding situations is one in each of its most tremendous skills. Many girls with ADHD learn how to cover their struggles well, regularly at great personal rate, in choice to expressing them in public. Being 'prepare' and 'ordinary' can take plenty of energy, that would bring about anxiety and a nagging feeling which you're not being understood.

The gender dynamics of ADHD also can be quite critical in relationships. Women with ADHD may additionally additionally experience particular troubles keeping near relationships. Their very traits, which make them lively and impulsive, might also furthermore struggle with social norms, leaving them feeling on my own and irritated. It will become vital for ladies with ADHD to talk brazenly on the way to offer an motive in the back of their wishes and problems and to construct empathy and knowledge of their relationships.

The gender dynamics of ADHD would probable provide opportunities and worrying situathons within the place of business. Women with ADHD may moreover make contributions unmatched resilience, creativity, and flexibility to their roles. It might be tough to strike a balance in place of work settings that fee conformity and order. The developments that set those women apart: hyperfocus, intuition, and a amazing factor of view may not align with conventional norms, necessitating a alternate in organizational manner of lifestyles so that you can virtually recognise their capability.

It's vital to understand that the consequences of ADHD on girls pass past the person and function an effect on social expectancies and perceptions. The big misconceptions round ADHD can purpose girls to battle longer earlier than receiving a prognosis and treatment, so that it will be broken with early intervention.

More and further humans have emerge as aware of the best issues confronted via ladies with ADHD in modern years. The tale is gradually changing as more activism and research spotlight the various methods that ADHD appears in first rate genders. As the gender dynamics of ADHD live untangled, it's miles becoming an increasing number of clean that embracing neurodiversity method honoring the awesome capabilities and viewpoints that all people, regardless of gender, brings to the table in addition to spotting versions.

In summary, the gender dynamics of ADHD provide an captivating framework for inspecting the diverse and often omitted reports of women handling this neurodevelopmental illness. We can foster a extra accepting and compassionate lifestyle that acknowledges and values the rich sort of the human mind by way of mastering approximately and valuing the nuanced subtleties of ADHD in ladies.

Recognizing Subtle Signs: Unmasking the Uniqueness

The intricacies of Attention Deficit Hyperactivity Disorder (ADHD) are regularly hard to find out in the large type of human research, mainly in women. Deciphering the peculiarities of ADHD in ladies requires a adventure of acknowledgment, comprehension, and recognition of the nuances that make this experience excellent. Think of it as solving a puzzle that famous the problematic fabric of specialty.

The Camouflaged Traits: Unveiling the Unseen

Women with ADHD regularly masks their signs and signs and symptoms with an invisible masks, hiding their condition below the floor. Contrary to the famous notion of hyperactive boys who can not prevent jumping off the partitions, girls with ADHD can also show off more subdued signs and symptoms. It's like a silent dance wherein the viewer does no longer right now choose out up at the beat.

Consider the exercise of having a pipe dream, as an instance. Though it is normally written off as a quick diversion, for women with ADHD, it is able to open doorways to a worldwide of creativity and mind. These daydreams are portals into a energetic mind that is continuously exploring new limitations, no longer actually diversion.

The Multitasking Maestros: Juggling with Grace

Women with ADHD are regularly the high-quality at multitasking in a society that celebrates it. But it is greater than without a doubt balancing obligations; it's far a complex ballet of concurrently handling obligations, thoughts, and mind. The delicacy is in knowledge a manner to go with the flow across this landscape of multitasking with such grace and simplicity that one can also moreover project an air of available beauty on the same time as the thoughts performs a complex symphony.

Imagine a female who runs a meeting, solutions emails, and plans the subsequent challenge with out issue; her mind movements rhythmically amongst severa duties, which might be best seemed to her.

This seemingly simple deed demonstrates the awesome approaches that ADHD gives itself in the enjoy of girls.

The Executive Function Conundrum: Navigating Life's Details

Women with ADHD frequently battle with government features, the cognitive techniques in fee of making plans, organizing, and being attentive to data. However, those problems might not be right away apparent. Rather, they seem subtly, together with sporadic forgetfulness or a chronic lack of ability to bear in thoughts everyday details.

Think approximately the woman who cautiously arranges her agenda, most effective to want to deal with unforeseen reroutes. It's a subtle tango with government functions that requires flexibility and resilience, now not a lack of art work or attentiveness. Understanding those nuances way appreciating the work required to hold the info below manage, even supposing the direction seems unsure.

Emotional Turbulence: Riding the Rollercoaster

ADHD in ladies is a complex circumstance that permeates many factors of the emotional landscape similarly to hobby and awareness. The nuance is in how feelings range, producing an emotional rollercoaster that won't be apparent inside the beginning. It's a succession of erratic weather styles as opposed to a non-stop hurricane.

Imagine a lady going about what appears to be a mean day, experiencing quick bursts of immoderate pride, frustration, and contemplated photo. Here, the complexity is inside the emotional size that offers the enjoy of female ADHD existence extra liveliness. Acknowledging the ones subtle emotional elements consists of accepting the rainbow of emotions that beautify the voyage.

Social Navigation: The Art of Connection

Social contacts may be charming and difficult for ladies with ADHD. The nuance is inside the dance of connection, wherein the urge to take part now and again collides with the issue of staying on project. It's about locating your very personal rhythm inside the social international, not approximately being detached.

Imagine a social event in which a lady with ADHD interacts with people resultseasily and every now and then suggests her wit. However, the nuance comes on the identical time as other topics in quick divert her attention and necessitate a cautious return to the social dance. Understanding the ones subtleties includes respecting the work required to establish lasting relationships no matter sporadic setbacks.

The Unseen Strengths: Celebrating the Uniqueness

Discovering the special traits of ADHD in girls includes extra than virtually declaring troubles—it moreover entails highlighting developments which may be frequently ignored. It's approximately appreciating the creativity that thrives inside the face of distraction, the tenacity that indicates up even as faced with problems with executive feature, and the emotional depth that enriches every come across.

Through this route of self-discovery, ladies with ADHD monitor a unique tapestry, woven with the threads of tiny signs and symptoms that distinguish their revel in as uniquely theirs. It's a voyage of self-discovery that delves past the obvious and invites a greater comprehension and appreciation of the nuances that mildew the tale of the woman ADHD.

Thus, preserve in mind that the following time you discover your self negotiating the complexities of ADHD, those complexities cover a story of fortitude, inventiveness, and energy. Exposing the uniqueness is a party of the super dance that distinguishes the revel in of female ADHD; it is more than most effective a voyage of self-interest.

Breaking Stereotypes: ADHD Beyond Hyperactivity

There is a common misperception within the huge region of ADHD that often obscures the complex reality: ADHD is not genuinely characterised through hyperactivity. In reality, the numerous women whose opinions with ADHD tackle various and difficult office work were harmed with the useful resource of this cartoon. So permit's were given all the way down to get to the lowest of this hyperactivity-centric concept and look at the complicated image of ADHD that lies

Chapter 11: Embarking On The Diagnostic Odyssey

Acknowledging Your ADHD Puzzle Pieces

Consider your life as a colourful mosaic of difficulties, research, and feelings, just like a jigsaw. Imagine now that there are precise quantities on this complex puzzle that, while you apprehend them, display a sample this is specific to you. This is the center of identifying the puzzle quantities that make up your ADHD: a self-discovery journey that turns reputedly unrelated bits right into a extra cohesive image of who you're.

Distracted moments are often at the same time as the number one piece of the puzzle comes collectively. Imagine an afternoon in which you have got been distracted and went off on tangents on the equal time as all of us else appeared to be targeted. Perhaps it took place at the equal time as analyzing a ebook, having a communicate with a friend, or perhaps subsequently of a commercial employer meeting. Even in the occasion that they do now not look like a whole lot, those little moments can show masses approximately how your mind functions. Identifying those occurrences is the initial degree in identifying when you have ADHD.

The perpetual jigsaw of thoughts in your head is every other trouble to observe. Have you ever had the effect that your thoughts were dancing vivaciously and feature a lifestyles of their non-public? This intellectual dance can be hard as well as creative for girls with ADHD. It's much like an never-ending brainstorming consultation on your head. When you word this as a problem of the puzzle, your intellectual method becomes more dynamic.

Another missing puzzle element is procrastination, this is regularly seen negatively. Think of a time at the same time as you struggled to cognizance and behind schedule beginning a assignment—now not because of the fact you have been being lazy. Those which have ADHD often undergo this. It's not that you're unmotivated; as a substitute, you are encountering specific troubles with the mind's government strategies. By viewing procrastination as a trouble of a bigger image, you may higher understand your behavior and devise answers.

Let's now observe the lacking aspect of hyperfocus. You have a examine successfully—hyperfocus. Even even though interest problems are often associated with ADHD, the ability to hyperfocus on thrilling subjects is an thrilling characteristic. Have you ever been so centered on a task that hours handed with out you information it? This 2nd of excessive popularity serves as a puzzle piece illustrating the depth and fervor that girls with ADHD might also additionally moreover deliver to their endeavors.

Another difficulty of the puzzle is furnished by way of using social interactions. Women with ADHD can also have once in a while observed it difficult to attention for the duration of social gatherings or to revel in out of rhythm with the communique. These are not signs and symptoms of indifference; instead, they may be illustrations of the superb way your brain translates data. Recognizing these social jigsaw portions lets in you to better recognize your communique fashion and forge stronger bonds with others.

It's worthwhile to investigate the time puzzle as nicely. Women who be with the aid of ADHD regularly war with the feeling that time is passing them with the aid of way of without warning. Have you ever miscalculated the quantity of time favored to finish a assignment or have become engrossed in an interest and misplaced song of time? These time-associated jigsaw quantities offer know-how of methods you relate to time and open the door to green time-control strategies customized for your necessities.

Take the organizational jigsaw piece for instance. It's no longer only approximately dropping your keys or skipping appointments; it is about coming up with unique, modern organizing techniques that provide you with the effects you need. Recognizing your private fashion of organizing offers you the capability to design structures that during shape your manner of questioning and way of lifestyles.

Let's finally remedy the enigma of emotional sensitivity. Elevated feelings are common in women with ADHD, beginning from excessive happiness to severe frustration. This emotional intensity is part of the puzzle that makes up your wonderful outlook on life. You may be given the complexity of your emotional opinions and create green coping mechanisms thru the usage of admitting your sensitivity.

To positioned it in reality, accepting the factors of your ADHD puzzle is a call to find out the rainbow of your evaluations. Distraction, hyperfocus, procrastination, or emotional sensitivity are only a few of the portions that make up the wonderful mosaic that is who you are. It's about appreciating the facts and peculiarities that make your puzzle distinctively yours, not about seeking to shoehorn it proper proper into a preconceived model. Thus, allow the approach of self-exploration to begin as you emerge as aware about, rate, and prepare the colourful puzzle quantities that make up your ADHD story.

Seeking Professional Guidance: The First Steps

Starting the gadget of having expert help for ADHD is like crusing on unknown waters with the hobby to emerge as a extra self-conscious man or woman. This first step is crucial; it's far a conscious preference to assist navigate the highbrow maze with the steering of seasoned professionals who concentrate on ADHD. Let's explore the nuances of these preliminary steps and turn what must look like a tough challenge into an exciting adventure of empowerment.

When you understand there may be some element unique about your studies that a professional will permit you to understand, it isn't always unusual to decide to are attempting to find expert suggest. Consider it as calling upon a reliable manual who is acquainted with the place and might offer insights which you can have neglected. Being inclined to research and be sincere approximately your emotions, ideas, and research is step one in the adventure.

Locating the perfect professional is one of the preliminary steps on this technique. It's just like choosing a experience partner: you want a person who can expertly navigate the terrain and recognize your dreams. On this journey, highbrow health experts specializing in ADHD, psychologists, and psychiatrists can function your guides. Seek for professionals focusing on person ADHD or, greater mainly, ADHD in ladies, because of the truth that this could guarantee an advanced comprehension of your terrific situation.

The approach usually starts offevolved with a communique as you interact with the ones specialists; the alternate feels each illuminating and adventurous. Think of it as having a verbal exchange with a mentor who in truth desires to concentrate approximately your revel in. They would possibly in all likelihood inquire approximately your upbringing, your interactions with others, and your critiques at paintings or college. Discovering your strengths, the tenacious threads woven within the course of your story, is truely as essential as overcoming the constraints.

The middle of getting expert advice is cooperation. It's a collaborative strive in that you offer your life tales and the expert applies their understanding to understand tendencies and subtleties. You may also embody individuals who are near you in this cooperation, together with family or pals, as they'll have tremendous viewpoints to make a contribution. It is similar to assembling a collection of reliable advisors, each contributing a jigsaw piece.

The diagnostic method itself is extra just like a communicate than a wondering. It's a place wherein you can test the subtleties of your stories and in which your mind are encouraged. Think of it like a painting consultation in that you and the artist collaborate to offer a canvas that captures the essence of your person revel in. They may moreover appoint masses of interviewing strategies and evaluation devices, however they may be devices to decorate statistics, now not barriers.

It's crucial to technique those exchanges with an open thoughts and self-compassion. This is prepared acquiring insights that empower you, not about labeling or passing judgment. The professional acts as a manual, presenting now not most effective a prognosis but additionally a path of motion. They assist you in deciphering the map through the usage of highlighting feasible aspect trips and picturesque paths that supplement your advantages and disadvantages.

To sum up, getting expert help for ADHD is a adventure of self-discovery, a planned research with the help of informed guides. Be open-minded, prepared to percentage your revel in, and enthusiastic about the upcoming cooperative voyage. Recall that this is approximately extra than clearly comprehending ADHD; it is approximately comprehending who you are, and the experts can help you see the manner in advance. So, revel in the journey of discovering the nuances of your private ADHD voyage and set sail with curiosity.

Collaborative Assessments: Crafting Your Personal Narrative

Collaborative exams grow to be an important a part of your very very own story inside the complicated technique of managing ADHD. This degree want to be viewed as a innovative partnership among you and the experts—a collectively-authored narrative that distills the middle of your evaluations, issues, and property.

Imagine your self inside the chair throughout from a intellectual fitness professional, with a pen symbolically for your hand to define the information of your lifestyles narrative. We are walking collectively that will help you apprehend the complexities of your enjoy with ADHD; this isn't just an assessment. The room is blank hold to your narrative, it absolutely is painted with wonder as you begin.

A mixture of dialogue, questions, and reflections are all part of the artwork of collaborative assessment. It is an research, corresponding to a creator exploring the boom of a protagonist's individual. You tackle the roles of each trouble and storyteller as you percentage anecdotes that interest the unique components of your critiques.

Like a careful editor, the expert listens with an expert ear, seeking out nuances and subtleties that assist create your story. This isn't a latest assessment; rather, it's miles a customized manner that recognizes the fact that everybody reminiscences ADHD in a one-of-a-kind way. Looking deeper into your past motives kids reminiscences to end up brushstrokes at the canvas of your enjoy with ADHD.

Chapter 12: Strategies For Daily Triumphs
Mastering Time: Techniques for Effective Management

This is the monetary catastrophe on time manipulate for your ADHD arsenal. Together, we are able to learn how to hold close time manipulate strategies that complement your mind's creative and dynamic character. Time is a blank canvas looking ahead on your ingenious strokes of manufacturing, no longer your enemy. Let's find out techniques which can be customized to the exceptional energy and sometimes mayhem that ADHD can supply, and that pass past common wondering.

1. Accept Your Superpower of Time-Tracking:

Start through redefining your statistics of the manner time is perceived. The great potential of ADHD minds to hyperfocus on topics that pique their hobby is common. Take gain of this abilties thru finding subjects to do that genuinely interest you. Discover the satisfaction in the system, and observe how time becomes an best friend in location of an enemy, whether or not it is a assignment at art work, a hobby, or in reality a home chore.

2. The Power of Small Goals:

Divide your day up into smaller objectives. Rather than struggling with the daunting concept of a long day, attention on small victories. Appreciate your accomplishments while you end every tiny mission thinking about the truth that they bring about a more a fulfillment and effective day.

three. Time blocking with a twist:

Traditionally, time blockading has concerned allocating particular obligations to predetermined time slots. Add a twist for the ADHD crowd. Permit a few wiggle room in every block. Go with the go along with the drift in case you had half of-hour set aside for emails however find out yourself out of place in a innovative second. Your friend in the combat for inexperienced time manage is adaptability.

four. Make Use of Outside Reminders:

A global whole of diversions may be navigated with the help of outdoor reminders. Make use of apps, sticky notes, or alarms that lightly remind you to move straight away to the following hobby. Reminders which might be externalized let you consciousness and reduce the risk that you will overlook vital chores.

five. The Method of Pomodoro:

Accept the Pomodoro Technique, a time-manipulate approach that divides work into periods of 25 mins every, interspersed with short pauses. This methodical method permits you avoid burnout on the same time as using your capability for hyperfocus. Try particular intervals to appearance what suits your personal rhythm the excellent.

6. Set Purpose-pushed priorities:

Understand that no longer each project is made equal. Establish sensible priorities via way of determining which responsibilities correspond collectively along with your average dreams. This isn't pretty loads time manipulate; it is also approximately allocating a while sensibly to hobbies that virtually pork up your profession and personal improvement.

7. Time Blocks for Routine Work:

Set apart precise time tablets for mundane or dull chores. Set apart a short quantity of time for positive duties, which encompass cleaning the house or answering regular emails. These chores should likely turn out to be lots less daunting and greater viable when there's a smooth endpoint in sight.

8. Time Management with Visuals:

Organize your day via using pics to their fullest functionality. Think about utilising thoughts maps, visible schedules, or colourful charts. Visual aids' vibrant and dynamic quality can inject some creativity into it slow control plan, growing its memorability and engagement.

9. Develop Strategic Rejection Skills:

Knowing your boundaries is a essential capacity for time control. Time is constrained, but your creativeness and exuberance are infinite. Develop strategic no-saying. Give top priority to duties with the intention to fulfill you and help you attain your dreams. Saying no on the identical time as it is essential is a self-care exercise and a crucial step on the direction to time control.

10. Reflect and Adjust:

Evaluate it sluggish control strategies on a ordinary foundation. What turn out to be effective? What desires to be changed? Continually comparing your self is vital to improving your approach. Accept the united statesand downs of experimenting and renowned that point control is a dynamic, ever-evolving capability.

When you're getting to know to master time, preserve in thoughts that the motive is to find out a rhythm that works along side your individual traumatic conditions and skills in preference to compelling yourself to match into predetermined preparations. Time is a canvas equipped to be painted along with your ingenuity and output. Accept the direction, widely recognized the accomplishments, and enjoy the ability of time manipulate in a way that speaks to the lively nature of your ADHD mind.

The Art of Organizing: Tailoring Methods to Your Style

Greetings from the dynamic place of organizing, an art work that actions to the beat of your very personal drumbeat. Learning the paintings of organizing for girls with ADHD is ready growing a symphony that suits your strength, fashion, and dynamic perception method, not just about cleaning up physical locations. Now absorb your conductor's baton and allow's take a look at out a way to customize organizational techniques to suit your specific composition.

Organizing is a non-public adventure that becomes woven into your normal lifestyles; it isn't always a one-length-suits-all shape of element. Think of organizing due to the fact the tremendous palette that adds harmony and order to the chaos of your painting, it's your lifestyles. The key's to adopt strategies that align at the side of your innate inclinations and strengths in preference to compelling yourself to in shape into inflexible systems.

Let's start via reading your top notch organizing method. Think of your mind as a kaleidoscope of standards, thoughts, and passions. Do you do first rate in an environment that is visually appealing and encourages creativity with patterns and shades? Or are you more of a minimalist, believing that minimalism encourages attention? Understanding your organizing fashion is the first step to growing a gadget that honestly works for you. Your organizing fashion is an extension of your individual.

If you revel in drawing concept from pictures, preserve in mind developing a imaginative and prescient board to feature a focal point in your targets and targets. Embrace pics, sayings, and turns on that inspire and power you. This concrete example of your desires offers your room a completely precise contact and acts as a dynamic road map for all your sports.Minimalism may be your compass if simplicity is your motto. Keep matters smooth with the beneficial useful resource of clearing out extraneous devices and specializing in what certainly topics. It can be liberating to stay with the aid of using the use of the "a lot much less is more" mentality, which lets you breathe in an surroundings with out vain distractions. Establish locations set out for unique duties so you may preserve matters prepared without tiring out your senses.

Let's now find out the vicinity of digital organizing, wherein technology can artwork for your gain. The way you put together chores, due dates, and thoughts is probably in reality changed with the aid of manner of apps and digital era. For the astute girl with ADHD who is also tech-savvy, check out productiveness equipment that during shape in collectively together with your workflow. Discover the virtual assistants that in form in properly together along with your ordinary normal, together with phrase-taking programs and mission managers.

The tactile experience of bodily planners and notebooks can be tempting to parents which might be tactile newcomers. Think of your diary as a private time pill in which you document your ideas, intentions, and reflections. Writing on paper may be recuperation because it creates a physical link amongst your thoughts and the web page.

Let's now talk the cadence of your day. Organizing is more than actually installing bodily areas; it's also planning your agenda. Take into hobby the use of time-blocking off techniques, in which you set up precise time slots for various responsibilities. By doing this, you can keep away from the maelstrom of distractions and keep rhythm with the day's sports. Schedule your sports activities sports to coincide collectively with your natural power peaks, whether or no longer you are a night time owl or a morning virtuoso.

Remember the charge of pliability as we traverse the organizing symphony. Because life is dynamic, your organizational techniques need to exchange as your research do. If the concept of "organized chaos" appeals in your innovative thing, encompass it. Occasionally, a chunk chaos comes before genius.

In the fantastic scheme of things, hold in thoughts that business enterprise is a technique in preference to a completely last purpose. Reward your self for tiny triumphs, decorate your techniques, and be privy to how your composition's melody changes through the years. By customizing organizational strategies to fit your non-public aesthetic, you could boom the regular into a piece of paintings that beautifully captures your energetic, dynamic essence. Thus, lead your symphony with satisfaction and allow the craft of arranging to transform into a melodious birthday celebration of your uniqueness.

Planning for Success: Strategies for Women with ADHD

Setting out on a path to achievement with ADHD is like seeking out your way spherical a hectic metropolis with all of its twists and turns. This adventure offers a wonderful set of possibilities and challenges for ladies with ADHD, and on this dynamic and constantly transferring terrain, properly-idea-out making plans becomes a reliable manual.

Let's begin thru redefining what planning in fact is. It's no longer approximately complex calendars with sunglasses assigned to each day or strict timetables. Rather, bear in thoughts planning as a dynamic dance, in which the rhythm adjustments steady together with your tempo and fashion. Recognize your alternatives and strengths first. Do you locate comfort in the written phrase, setting down mind and dreams, or are you a visible philosopher who does awesome with mind maps and diagrams?

Knowing your very very own planning possibilities will assist you create strategies that fit your manner of questioning. If you are pinnacle with snap shots, do not forget making vision boards or employing device that will can help you visually constitute your goals in an attention grabbing and fun way. If your buddies are terms, then a digital be conscious-taking tool or a well organized diary can be your reliable accomplice.

Additionally, encompass the electricity of chunking, that is the department of exertions into digestible, manageable additives. Consider your self confronted with a hard conundrum; in search of to figure all of it out right away can be disturbing. Divide it into extra digestible, smaller chunks, and experience the gratification of completing each one. This method takes under consideration the eye span fluctuations that every so often accompany ADHD in addition to encouraging a sense of fulfillment.

One vital remarkable pal in this dynamic planning technique is flexibility. Because existence is basically unpredictable, it will become an artwork for girls with ADHD to embody the ebb and drift. Include flexibility on your plans to address closing-minute changes and spontaneity. The goal is to create a framework that gracefully handles the sudden in place of implementing anxiety.

Making a photograph of your path to success is another effective tactic. Imagine the surrender cease result, however revel in the journey as properly. By encouraging a effective outlook and reaffirming your self-control to the road ahead, visualization permits you get right of entry to the motivating force that is your mind. It's similar to developing a highbrow movie in that you play the strong lead individual who overcomes boundaries with creativeness and tenacity.

Chapter 13: Navigating Emotional Waters

Managing Anxiety and Stress: A Woman's Perspective

Anxiety and stress can often take center level in the tumultuous dance of existence, in particular for girls negotiating the dynamic difficulties of the cutting-edge global. See it as an problematic tapestry with the strands representing responsibilities, requirements, and the sporadic curveballs existence offers you. It becomes an artwork to control tension and strain; it is a remarkable balancing act that calls for a combination of resilience, self-recognition, and self-compassion.

This tapestry might seem loads extra complicated to girls who be bothered through ADHD. It's just like taking walks a tightrope, a immoderate-stakes act at the same time as placing the right balance between everyday obligations and private nicely-being is wanted. But this intricacy also provides a risk for improvement and empowerment.

Let's find out the subtleties of pressure and tension manipulate from the attitude of a girl. Imagine yourself because of the truth the compass, gracefully navigating thru the usaand downs of the journey.

Handling the Anxiety Waves

Often, tension enters your lifestyles all of sudden and faucets on your shoulder at the same time as you least count on it to. Being a girl may additionally require you to balance a number of obligations, which incorporates children, relationships, and your artwork. The first step is knowing that fear is a everyday reaction to life's needs in preference to a sign of weak spot. It's much like understanding that waves come and pass inside the water and which you should learn how to adventure them with fortitude.

Accepting Stress as a Growth-Catalyst

Stress can act as a catalyst for increase, in loads of strategies strain can turn coal right into a diamond. From a lady attitude, it's miles approximately redefining stress as something that allows you move beforehand. Think about pressure because the wind pushing you to gain new heights. This change in angle can permit you to method obstacles with a feeling of cause, using strain as a springboard in place of a roadblock.

Creating Your Stress-Reduction Resource Kit

Consider relieving stress as setting together your very non-public custom designed toolkit. It's a hard and fast of strategies catered in your tastes as opposed to a single, regularly happening solution. Every tool adds a layer of resilience, whether or not it is taking comfort in nature, developing artwork, or working towards mindfulness. This toolset will become your hidden weaponry as an ADHD girl, equipped to be used on every occasion stress comes knocking.

Building a Self-Compassionate Culture

Women regularly ought to balance the need to be the extraordinary at the entirety within the speedy-paced worldwide of expectations. Building a subculture of self-compassion is essential, like tending a lawn wherein compassion and know-how flourish. Consider your self to be in want of the same help which you might provide a friend. It's much like tending a delicate flower, wherein each petal stands for a first rate issue of your character direction, nourished thru the smooth rain of self-love.

Creating Connections: The Influence of Common Experiences

Women are manifestly true at connecting with others, and this trait in reality suggests nearly about strain and anxiety manipulate. Think of it as a circle of assist wherein understanding is woven collectively by manner of manner of shared stories. Speak with loved ones, buddies, or perhaps distinct woman ADHD patients. By sharing your reviews and presenting assist, you may create a protection internet of connections to help you cope with strain in a set setting.

In end, from a woman's mind-set, managing pressure and tension is an art work that calls for accepting, reinterpreting, and spotting life's intricacies. Keep in thoughts which you are the most effective maintaining the comb to shade the canvas of your revel in as you undergo the severa steps of this experience. Resilience, self-compassion, and network resource can assist you turn the tumultuous tapestry into a chunk of grace and electricity.

Riding the Emotional Rollercoaster: Regulating Feelings

When you've got ADHD, navigating the emotional terrain is much like the use of a rollercoaster—it is able to be thrilling, unpredictable, and every so often overpowering. This financial ruin will take a look at the complexities of emotion law and provide tips and strategies that will help you have a extra snug emotional adventure.

Visualize the colours of your feelings as motors on the ADHD rollercoaster. You could be ecstatic one minute after which, in the region of some seconds, you locate your self descending right proper into a state of excessive dissatisfaction or impatience. The first step to taming this emotional rollercoaster is to understand it.

Elevated emotional sensitivity is a energy and a war for lots ladies with ADHD. Because of your eager emotional feel, you're capable of honestly have interaction with human beings and recognize life's many blessings. It moreover implies that there can be exhilarating highs and miserable lows, just like plunging proper into a stormy sea.

Let's start with the climb, the exciting peaks. Savoring the moment is important even as you're feeling precise about yourself. No depend how modest your victory changed into, have a amazing time it and experience the exceptional energy coursing via you. Turn those moments into shared research that deepen your relationships with people spherical you by using using spreading your pleasure to them.

And now for the downs: the tough abysses. While it's suitable to revel in horrible feelings to a excessive degree, it's also crucial to look at coping mechanisms for those low factors. Think of it like collectively with brakes and protection harnesses on your rollercoaster. Mindfulness is one beneficial tool. Just prevent, inhale, and spend a second looking your feelings without passing judgment. If you try this small, but powerful motion, you may get better manipulate inside the event that the rollercoaster suddenly dips.

Taking element in sports that make you sense glad and comfortable is every other approach. Engaging in a favorite interest, taking vicinity a nature stroll, or sipping a relaxing cup of tea are examples of sports activities sports that act as stabilizers and assist to balance out the emotional curler coaster. Think of them as your very personal set of equipment for controlling your feelings.

Navigating the americaand downs of the emotional rollercoaster related to ADHD calls for effective communication. Let near pals or circle of relatives people realise the way you sense as a way to empathize with you. Expressing your feelings is a electricity that promotes help and connection in place of a sign of prone thing.

Let's now speak loop-de-loops, or the ones instances where feelings appear to get out of manage. The process of proactive emotional law involves spotting triggers and placing preventative measures in vicinity.

Acknowledge tendencies for your emotional rollercoaster and equip yourself with techniques to confront barriers head-on.

Finally, see the opportunities for boom in the loop-the-loops. Every turn gives an opportunity to growth as someone and hone your emotional manipulate talents. It's approximately turning the rollercoaster right into a resilient and self-discovering journey in vicinity of a crazy experience.

Managing the emotional rollercoaster associated with ADHD is accepting every turn as part of your individual route, spotting your highs and lows, and placing regulating techniques into exercising. You might also additionally flip the rollercoaster into an enjoy that enhances in desire to depletes your existence thru deliberately and resiliently coping with your feelings.

Tapping into Resilience: Emotional Strengths of Women with ADHD

Women with ADHD weave resilient threads in the colourful tapestry of life, each with its very very own tremendous colorations and textures. These people are a long way from being described absolutely with the useful resource in their struggles; in addition they've a robust set of emotional dispositions that permit them to flourish specifically strategies at the same time as moreover letting them climate tough conditions.

Among the diverse splendid traits, adaptability sticks out. Imagine a girl with ADHD gliding through the ever-converting rhythms of existence like a nimble dancer. Their superpower becomes their capability to evolve, which permits them to deal with uncertainty with fashion and originality. When conditions alternate, the ones girls use their innate adaptability to show boundaries into possibilities for development.

A sturdy experience of empathy is definitely one more gem inside the crown of emotional strengths. Women with ADHD regularly have a sixth enjoy for emotions, both their very personal and special people's. They seem to possess a certainly touchy emotional radar that allows them to empathize intensely with others spherical them. This empathetic understanding cultivates deep and lasting connections, building a network of beneficial useful resource that grows stronger.

Innate treatment is any other deliver of resilience. Imagine it as a ferocious electricity that doesn't permit barriers to quench it. When confronted with stressful situations, ladies with ADHD find an internal supply of electricity that maintains them moving ahead with unyielding choice. This perseverance makes even the tiniest successes look like enormous achievements, which feeds a experience of fulfillment.

A incredible brushstroke inside the emotional strengths palette is creativity. Women with ADHD regularly have vibrant imaginations and the functionality for unconventional idea. This inventiveness stimulates creativity and hassle-fixing, turning obstacles into opportunities for progressive expression. It resembles having a regular deliver of proposal that illuminates their direction.

Moreover, a sense of humor that dances in the face of misfortune is intricately related to resilience. Humor is a exceptional tool that women with ADHD regularly use to transform normal mishaps into humorous narratives. This playful technique releases stress and brings satisfaction into their existence, providing a contemporary day outlook on the adventure of living with ADHD.

Understanding the significance of connection inside the emotional strengths of girls with ADHD is crucial. They are adept at developing and preserving deep connections that promote a feel of belonging and guide. This connection becomes a crucial resilience pillar, supplying a defend in trying instances and an area to have an outstanding time in a fulfillment ones.

Women with ADHD add vivid hues of perseverance, flexibility, empathy, willpower, creativity, and humor to the stunning material of existence. These emotional strengths are the crucial thread that connects their man or woman lives; they may be not without a doubt extras. Let's encompass the deep resilience that characterizes the journey of women with ADHD as we recognize and have a good time the ones developments. This adventure is characterized with the resource of bravery, inventiveness, and an unyielding spirit that in no way fails to inspire us all.

Chapter 14: Relationships And Communication

Love, Connection, and ADHD: Impact on Intimate Relationships

Navigating the panorama of ADHD can highlight both remarkable characteristics and specific boundaries in the complicated dance of affection and relationships. Imagine dancing a passionate waltz with a companion, with every stride signifying the careful balancing act among the flurry of mind and emotions that could accompany ADHD and connection. Let's take a look at how ADHD impacts close relationships and check the threads that bind love together.

Above all, it is critical to understand that having ADHD does no longer define someone or restriction their capability to love. Rather, it adds a completely precise tempo to the intimacy dance, one which necessitates mutual synchronization among lovers. In any courting, conversation is important, and in phrases of ADHD, it takes on a inclined and information dance.

It may be tough for people with ADHD to as it ought to be express and modify their feelings. Imagine trying to speak the nuances of your feelings at the same time as your thoughts is a busy market complete with ideas, distractions, and mind. It's like attempting to tell a story in the center of a hectic carnival; it's tough but conceivable.

This trouble can show up in some of strategies, which incorporates occasional trouble focusing on the current second, impulsivity, or forgetfulness. A accomplice might also moreover enjoy a rollercoaster experience as they navigate the highs and lows of forgetfulness and spontaneity. It's approximately gaining knowledge of to ride the waves collectively, no longer approximately now not having love or dedication.

Promoting honest and nonjudgmental verbal exchange is vital to controlling the results of ADHD on relationships. A stable place wherein both sports can speak their needs, frustrations, and joys ought to be created through the use of the usage of companions. Consider it as growing a commonplace language that allows you to each realise the little versions in every specific's reviews.

For people with ADHD, keeping interest in the course of intimate moments may be hard. Imagine a associate whose thoughts is type of a busy town square, with a lot taking vicinity at once that it is hard to pay attention on surely one thing. However, there may be a superb beauty hidden inside the center of this colourful turmoil. Partners can learn how to cost the actual excitement, innovative outbursts, and spontaneity that ADHD can carry to a courting.

In the within the period in-between, developing shape and workout routines turns into essential for supporting couples deal with ADHD. Instead of suppressing spontaneity, the intention is to gather a robust basis that permits every companions to be successful. Picture a lawn in which ADHD wildflowers are allowed to broaden freely, but there are also borders and paths that provide form and direction.

The effect of ADHD on the department of responsibilities in a relationship is each other detail to maintain in mind. Sometimes impulsivity and forgetfulness bring about an imbalance of obligations and obligations. See a partnership wherein each activities actively art work together to find out practicable solutions, in desire to frustration. Finding a balanced art work branch that capitalizes on each companion's blessings is the important issue.

In fact, in terms of relationships stricken by ADHD, patience will become a special function. Imagine it as a revel in that both spouses take together, analyzing and developing as a set. Even if there may be setbacks along the road, the self-control to comprehending, encouraging, and taking factor in every other makes the dance right into a lovely, if erratic, masterpiece.

Partner schooling concerning ADHD will become an powerful device as they set off on this path. It's similar to having a guidebook that makes the turns and turns less difficult to understand. Participate in open discussions that promote understanding, have a look at approximately ADHD as a collection, and attend workshops together.

ADHD offers fantastic colorings and complex patterns to the love tapestry, wherein every thread enhances the beauty of the entire. It's now not a weakness however alternatively a completely unique brushstroke that gives a partnership greater persona and nuance. Accept the dance, enjoy the oddities, and bask inside the love that surpasses the subtleties of ADHD. In the huge ballroom of life, notwithstanding the whole thing, each partner's very non-public beat is what certainly elevates the dance.

Navigating Communication: Expressing Your ADHD Experience

Communicating approximately your enjoy with ADHD and navigating conversation is like weaving your personal thoughts, feelings, and views right right into a colorful tapestry. It's an paintings, a ballet of phrases that creates a superb picture of your adventure with ADHD, not only a rely of delivering facts. Together, permit's set out on this expressive journey to research the subtleties of speaking your enjoy with readability, sincerity, and likely a hint of comedy.

Chapter 15: Understanding Adhd

The Neuroscience in the back of ADHD

Imagine a bustling city: cars racing down highways, pedestrians navigating sidewalks and lights flickering among skyscrapers. Each element--vehicles, pedestrians and lighting fixtures alike--represents part of your thoughts working harmoniously together. Now recollect that once ADHD sets in movement its traffic lights at intersections may additionally malfunction inflicting collisions more frequently; crossing pedestrians discover it harder to move streets ensuing in reduced normal standard performance of each town (aka mind) and mind function modern day.

ADHD can be described scientifically as an alteration to neural activity and mind shape. Neurotransmitters together with dopamine and norepinephrine, which assist facilitate communique among neurons, have reduced availability or behave in unpredictable methods. These chemicals play a crucial function in authority's functions: talents had to manage regular life duties like concentrating, organizing and starting tasks. Neurotransmitters act like net web page traffic lights that help coordinate interest during your thoughts whilst those neurotransmitters do not function effectively then pathways relying on them battle to perform optimally.

Let's dive deeper. Imagine being assigned a task at paintings; under everyday situations, your prefrontal cortex--known as the 'command center'--would possibly set off an extensive chain of cognitive sports activities sports designed to finish it successfully: prioritizing obligations, strategizing to satisfy them efficaciously, allocating property accurately, and filtering out functionality distractions earlier than beginning artwork on it.

Imagine Sarah is a advertising and advertising supervisor with ADHD. Upon receiving a trendy project, her brain struggles with its obligations the website traffic lights that should help direct her concept manner do not continuously characteristic efficiently, leaving her often sidetracked or fixated on minute data which include font desire in region of fundamental content advent Or worse despite the fact that jumping in with out cautious attention only to come to be mired down later and unmanageable due to inconsistent neurotransmitter hobby in her government features.

Her inner town is in chaos because of unsteady neurotransmitter interest governing authorities capabilities which govern government functions like authorities competencies dominated via government talents ruled through neurotransmitter interest it simply is hardwired into manage by way of manner of using the ones govt abilties being managed 'internet page visitors lights'

What reasons neurotransmitter fluctuations? Genetic elements play an important trouble, with research indicating ADHD has an expected heritability estimate of 70-80%; therefore if one same twin has ADHD then there can be a 70-80% danger that his or her equal sibling additionally does; environmental factors in some unspecified time in the destiny of prenatal and childhood levels collectively with exposure to alcohol or tobacco in utero, low begin weight or excessive lead tiers of their our bodies also boom the possibilities of ADHD development.

Brain form plays a significant feature in ADHD symptoms. Studies the use of magnetic resonance imaging (MRI) have found out that human beings with ADHD regularly show variations in excessive great areas, like their prefrontal cortex which frequently becomes smaller this area controls executive functions which will be inclined to grow to be impaired in people residing with ADHD. Research is now being performed at the way to map the ones structural versions more exactly as a way to format extra inexperienced remedy plans.

ADHD gives an interesting interrelation amongst its symptoms and signs and circadian rhythm. Individuals dwelling with ADHD frequently find their inner body clock off-kilter, crucial to troubles slumbering at ordinary times an critical requirement for cognitive abilties and absence of that can exacerbate ADHD signs and signs and symptoms similarly. People residing with ADHD can regularly have trouble sound asleep in the course of traditional bedtime hours which influences alertness and recognition in the morning.

Take Mark, an ADHD freelance writer. His most green hours lie among middle of the night and 4 AM at the identical time as most others sleep; however this unusual time table impacts on his daylight commitments; morning conferences frequently display difficult, even as remaining dates that require going for walks in some unspecified time in the future of preferred enterprise hours often bypass him via unfinished. ADHD intertwines with different physiological strategies to similarly complicate man or woman experiences.

New breakthroughs in neuroscience are also imparting greater readability into the plasticity of the mind, its ability for neural pathways to reconfigure themselves. ADHD is not seen as an unchanging condition but as a neurodevelopmental infection with room for development. Medication like methylphenidate and amphetamines or non-stimulant options on the facet of atomoxetine can assist stability neurotransmitter ranges to some extent thereby "solving" internet site site visitors lighting fixtures that have malfunctioned; behavioral remedy works hand in hand with the ones techniques in hopes of building extra green neural networks.

Understanding ADHD neuroscience is like dissecting an complex metropolis. Neurotransmitter hobby and mind shape, genetic elements and environmental affects in addition to govt features and sleep patterns all comprise one piece of this puzzle; and as more is located with modern-day technologies and research methodologies the picture turns into ever clearer. Our goal have to be to use this developing information into increasingly powerful treatments and interventions designed to optimize every individual metropolis so life becomes viable but tremendous for the ones living with ADHD.

Unique Challenges for Women

To recognize ADHD in girls, visualize an hard tapestry. Each thread represents some element of her existence--from profession and relationships to her health and personal happiness. When we add ADHD into this cloth, however, the threads also can begin unraveling as signs and symptoms and symptoms and signs emerge in a exquisite manner than they could in men; hormone fluctuations, social expectations and motherhood all play a difficulty. To fully understand this complicated net of signs we need to explore numerous domain names which includes gender-particular signs and symptoms and signs similarly to hormonal fluctuations and motherhood issues.

When discussing ADHD from a gender standpoint, it is critical to maintain in mind that diagnostic criteria were initially evolved the use of studies completed particularly with extra youthful guys; as a quit end result, ADHD in women has lengthy long long gone undetected. Women commonly show signs in some other manner from male contrary numbers: lots much less hyperactivity and more inattentiveness making their situation tons much less complicated to transport undiagnosed. Imagine Emily, an undergraduate university scholar who has no longer been identified with ADHD due to the fact she does not disrupt instructions. Emily unearths it tough to popularity on lectures or readings, misplacing property frequently, and regularly drifting off into daydreams. Such inattentive signs and symptoms and symptoms might also need to without troubles be misattributed to person tendencies instead of neurological conditions similarly delaying evaluation and treatment.

Hormones add a few one of a kind degree of complexity. Estrogen, which controls dopamine release, plays an important thing. Any fluctuation of estrogen degrees all through menstruation cycles, pregnancy and menopause can intensify ADHD symptoms. Laura is in her overdue 40s who has lived with ADHD her entire lifestyles. During menopause her symptoms and signs worsen further as estrogen stages drop inflicting trouble with attention, emotional regulation or perhaps forgetfulness to increase. These aren't honestly "menopausal signs", those are ADHD exacerbated by hormonal adjustments.

Women living with ADHD face specific societal expectations at the identical time as performing roles requiring multitasking and emotional exertions. Primary caregivers or professionals balancing art work and domestic life also can find out the govt feature deficits associated with ADHD debilitating. Megan, as an instance, who holds down each a whole-time technique in addition to being a mother to a few more youthful youngsters reveals retaining song of clinical health practitioner's appointments, college sports activities sports and own family chores can experience like seeking to stability more than one balls concurrently at the same time as preserving her cool beneath pressure from society's expectancies exacerbates her challenges in addition inclusive of societal expectancies that upload layers of guilt or disgrace for no longer retaining her cool underneath stress.

Motherhood can be an uphill struggle for women with ADHD. From emotional stressful conditions related to being concerned for a child to logistical hurdles like feeding schedules or dealing with college exercising workouts, ADHD symptoms make the duties even greater difficult. Sarah, a ultra-cutting-edge mom with ADHD signs finds it hard to stick to her new baby's feeding and sleeping schedule due to ADHD signs and symptoms and signs and symptoms inflicting disruptions that every have an impact on her health and that of her toddler, fundamental to strain that worsens ADHD symptoms in addition.

Women diagnosed with ADHD are at an advanced danger for anxiety and despair. Psychological stressors because of continuously struggling to suit in or years of undiagnosed symptoms affecting shallowness can exacerbate the ones conditions further. Lisa, diagnosed in her 30s, spent some years believing her issues at college and later paintings were because of some intrinsic flaw in herself, fundamental her into tension attacks in addition to avoidance behaviors which compromised performance throughout wonderful lifestyles domain names.